AVOIDING DECEPTION

AVOIDING DECEPTION

by
Sharon Daugherty

Unless otherwise indicated, all Scripture quotations are taken from the *King James Version* of the Bible.

All Scripture quotations marked AMP are taken from *The Amplified Bible, New Testament,* copyright © 1958, 1987 by The Lockman Foundation, La Habra, California, or *The Amplified Bible, Old Testament,* copyright © 1964, 1987 by Zondervan Publishing House, Grand Rapids, Michigan.

All Scripture quotations marked NASB are taken from the *New American Standard Bible.* Copyright © 1960, 1962, 1963, 1968, 1971, 1972, 1973, 1975, 1977 by The Lockman Foundation, La Habra, California.

All Scripture quotations marked NIV are taken from *The Holy Bible: New International Version.* Copyright © 1973, 1978, 1984 by The International Bible Society. Used by permission of Zondervan Bible Publishers.

All Scripture quotations marked NKJV are taken from the *New King James Version* of the Bible. Copyright © 1979, 1980, 1982, Thomas Nelson, Inc., Publishers.

All Scripture quotations marked TLB are taken from *The Living Bible.* Copyright © 1971, 1988 by Tyndale House Publishers, Inc., Wheaton, Illinois.

Avoiding Deception
ISBN 1-56267-157-X
Copyright © 1997 by
Sharon Daugherty
Victory Christian Center
7700 South Lewis Avenue
Tulsa, OK 74136-7700
Second printing, June 1997

CONTENTS

FOREWORD

Avoiding Deception touches a critical area of need in the Body of Christ. This message must be heard, for millions are being blinded by the powers of darkness.

Sharon speaks from her heart on the issue of deception. She has heard from God concerning what people must do to avoid being deceived. Weekly, we minister to people who are coming out of deception. She has over twenty-four years of firsthand, one-on-one experience guiding people into freedom.

Sharon is a wonderful wife to me and the joyful mother of four children. Our two girls and two boys are saved, Spirit filled and serving God. Daily, Sharon is seeking God's help in her own life to fulfill her call as a witness for Jesus, a wife, a mother, a co-pastor, teacher in the Bible school, worship leader, and author.

This is an eye-opening book for those who are unaware of the last days' deceptions. For some the message will make the difference between heaven or hell. All of us need God's help to walk in the light. As you read these words, get ready for the darkness to flee.

Billy Joe Daugherty

INTRODUCTION

What causes a Christian man or woman to leave what appears to be a solid marriage of several years for an affair with another person which costs them everything (children, finances, friends, job and reputation)?

What causes someone to begin feeding their mind on pornography (R- and X-rated television programs, movies and videos), magazines and books, thinking that as long as they hide it, it's okay? What causes a father to molest his daughter secretly, thinking he'll never be caught? What causes someone to let their anger explode and physically abuse their family members, blaming their circumstances or their family members for it?

What causes someone to believe that, though he or she was created physically one way, instead they are the opposite sex? What causes someone to habitually lie about everything in order to cover up what they don't want others to know? What makes them fear being honest with people? Why do they think that lying will actually gain them position, friends, financial increase, or a better life?

What causes someone, who desires to be a leader, to gather a few followers and then begin to control their lives, isolating them from others who might expose the deception of this leader? What causes someone to quit the church, quit reading their Bible, quit praying and quit doing what is right? What causes someone to blame everyone else and never examine their own hearts? What causes Christians to quit church and think they can survive without a relationship or fellowship with other Christians?

Introduction

All of these questions have one answer. Deception!
Webster defines *deceived* as "to believe what is false or
invalid to be true or valid; to be misled; or to be
ensnared."[1] He defines *deceive* as "to deliberately mis-
represent facts by works or actions *in order to further
one's own interests*." Other words related in meaning
include *beguile*, "to entice a prospect by giving them
promises of gaining something for going along with the
plan of action"; *mislead*, "to cause to follow the wrong
course"; *delude*, "to fool someone so completely that he
or she accepts what is false to be true"; *fraud*, "a deliberate deception in dishonestly depriving a person of property, rights, etc."; *betray*, "a breaking of faith while
appearing to be loyal."[2] Each of the examples mentioned
previously falls into one or more of these categories of
definition.

The adulterer is enticed or entices someone by giving
the person promises of gaining a more exciting relationship for going along with their plan of action. They also
break their word and covenant made with another person
while appearing to be loyal. A lie is told in order to cover
up their wrong. An old cliche says, "The grass always
looks greener on the other side of the fence," but after
you get there, you'll find some unexpected thorns. Also,
an unfaithful person will reap unfaithfulness later on
from the seeds he or she sows into a relationship they
think they have gained, but which has been built in a

---

[1] *Merriam Webster's Collegiate Dictionary*, Tenth Ed., Springfield, MA:
Merriam-Webster, Inc., 1996, p. 298.
[2] *Webster's New World Dictionary*, New York, NY: Simon & Schuster,
1982. (*Deceive*, p. 196; *beguile*, p. 67; *mislead*, p. 479; *delude*, p. 200;
fraud, p. 298; *betray*, p. 71.)

wrong manner.

The pornographer is enticed and misled, thinking the mental excitement he believes he gets doesn't hurt anyone. Wrong! All sin first begins as a thought. If a thought is meditated upon, it will become an action. Jesus said, "If you even think of committing sexual sin in your heart, it is already sin" (Matthew 5:28). It must be repented of and the source of it cut off. First Thessalonians 5:23 says we are to *avoid* every appearance of evil. Get away from it. Go another direction to escape its influence.

Someone who commits incest against another has misrepresented facts to further his or her own interests. They cause their victim to follow the wrong course of action as they proceed to violate them sexually. The victim believes that if he or she tells, they will get hurt. But instead, if they would reveal the truth, they would go free and the victimizer would be made to face responsibility for his or her actions.

The physical abuser makes his or her victim believe what is not truth to be truth by telling them they are the cause of the abuse when, in reality, the abuser has never submitted his or her will and emotions to God and brought them into self-control.

The homosexual or lesbian has allowed an unclean desire to become so strong that instead of resisting it, they've convinced themselves to believe what is not truth to be truth in order to further their own lust.

The liar deceives people into believing what is not truth to be truth to further his or her own interests and appears to be loyal while misleading all the way.

In the sphere of the church, the deceiver who desires a position of spiritual leadership misleads and misrepresents facts, usually not telling everything so as not to reveal themselves. Normally, they make others in leadership appear wrong or lacking in some way, believing they have all the answers, in order to further their own interests. Sometimes they deprive people of property and rights saying it is for the benefit of everyone that they do this when it is for their own benefit.

Christians who stop reading the Word of God and praying daily open themselves up to deception. Also, those who are not actively involved and rightly related to leadership and members within a church, as well as giving out of their lives to God and others, will expose themselves to the devil's deception. They have misled themselves, thinking they know enough to coast into heaven.

There are many other examples I could give. These are just a few of the deceptions people are facing in the world today. How a Christian recognizes and responds to Satan's tactics can determine his or her eternal destiny.

Throughout the New Testament, the Scriptures warn us not to become deceived. If a Christian could not ever become deceived, then Jesus would not have warned us "not to become deceived." Paul and James would not have written it in their letters to the churches. (Note: One characteristic of the last days is **"...evil men and seducers shall wax worse and worse, deceiving and being deceived"** (2 Timothy 3:13). We're living in what 2 Timothy 3:1 calls "perilous times" of the last days. It is also a time of the Holy Spirit being poured out upon the earth in every nation, and multitudes are being saved and filled with the Holy Spirit. (See Joel 2:28; Acts 2:17; Matthew 24:14.) Please let your heart be open to receive what I believe God is trying to alert Christians about in this crucial hour.)

One night in the month of January, 1990, I was abruptly awakened out of my sleep. There was no natural reason for me to be awakened. (Since I am a very sound sleeper, it was not normal for me to wake up in the middle of the night.) I knew immediately that it was the Lord Who had awakened me, and I was wide awake as if an alarm had gone off. However, no alarm had gone off! I arose from the bed. My family members were all sound asleep.

Within my spirit, I heard the voice of God so strong that even though it wasn't an audible voice, it could have been. He said to me, "You've wondered how the elect could ever be deceived. You've wondered how people, who are members of strong churches that preach the whole counsel of the Word of God, people who seemingly appear to be stable Christians, could ever be deceived in the last days." He said, "I'm going to show you."

He spoke to my heart, "You are entering the last of the last days as you enter the 1990s." He said, "You will see some Christians who appear to be established and faithful church attenders fall away from Me. Some will be restored by recognizing their sin and repenting. Others will become hardened, rejecting repentance. Their lives will be destroyed, but worst of all, they'll go to hell." He then showed me four basic ways people would become deceived. Neglect of:

• The Word
• Prayer
• Right-Relatedness
• Giving out of their lives.

(We will cover each of these four areas in separate chapters of this book.) Amazingly, these are the four simple areas that ministers teach new converts on how to grow in their Christian lives.

I was so shaken within me over this experience because I had a godly fear or alarm regarding people I knew, as well as the entire Body of Christ. I shared this experience with my husband, and he felt it needed to be shared immediately with our own body of believers. After that, each place I was asked to speak, I shared what God had spoken within my spirit. Over these past few years, He has shown me more regarding what He spoke to me that night.

Isaiah 60:1-3 says though gross darkness will cover the face of the earth, God's glory will come upon the Church (Zion) and multitudes will be drawn to the brightness of His rising. In these last days two things are transpiring. Much darkness (sin, crime, destruction, pain, heartache, etc.) is happening around the world, yet God is also moving in the greatest outpouring of His Holy Spirit in all of history, bringing in the last days' harvest.

It is exciting to see what God is doing. However, we cannot close our eyes to the darkness and think we will not have to face it, confront it and bring the light of the Gospel into it. Second Thessalonians 2:1-3 even says for us not to be deceived. Before Jesus returns there will be some Christians who fall away from walking with Him. Jesus said as iniquity or sin abounds, some Christians will wax cold in their love for Him (Matthew 24:12).

This is why I am so compelled to write and encourage believers to be sober and alert. While we are receptive to the wonderful workings of the Holy Spirit, we must also listen and be watchful in this hour. The well-being in our own lives, as well as the the salvation of other people, is dependent on how spiritually alert we are.

I believe if we can guard our hearts from losing our fervent love for Jesus and His Word and maintain a servant heart, we can keep ourselves. We can also help keep those we are called to influence from becoming cold, lukewarm, or hardened.

As you read the following pages, I pray that God will speak to your heart. If things are right in your life, I pray that you will sense the same urgency of the hour we are in and will reach out and help others to see. If things are not right in your life, I pray you'll be able to make the changes needed to prepare yourself for the soon coming of Jesus Christ.

WHERE DID DECEPTION BEGIN?

*L*et's first examine *where deception began.*
Revelation 20:3 tells us that Satan is the
deceiver of the nations. We see in Isaiah 14:12-
15 and Ezekiel 28:12-19 that Satan (Lucifer) was a created being who God had created as an archangel to lead
worship in heaven. Satan was created with musical
instruments within his very being. But Satan began to
desire the position of God to lead. He desired the service
and admiration of others. This is where pride entered his
heart. (Anyone who leads out of jealousy and pride will
fall from their position. Any gathering around them will
be a small group and will be controlled by them.)

Obadiah verse 3 says, **"The pride of thine heart
hath deceived thee...."** *Immediately Satan and a third of
the angels who followed him were cast down from heav-
en.* This created chaos or confusion for a moment and
order had to be restored. Some theologians believe this is
why Genesis 1:1 has the statement of creation, and then
Genesis 1:2 says the earth was without form and void
and darkness covered the face of the earth. In the midst
of all of this, the Spirit of the Lord *moved* over the face
of the earth. God began to speak order into the chaos. He
called forth every living thing into existence. (Note: God
will never let confusion and darkness have the final say.

> *He [God] is always moving by His Spirit to counter and outdo the enemy.*

He is always moving by His Spirit to counter and outdo the enemy.)

Satan didn't give up. After creation he came to the garden of Eden. He knew if he could deceive mankind he could come against God Who had cast him down. In Genesis 3, you could say that Satan waited until Adam (the husband, the protector and garden keeper) was preoccupied or spiritually asleep. (As Christians, we must stay awake spiritually so the enemy can be recognized and kept out when he tries to come.) Satan then appealed to the lack of discernment in Eve, her desire to know more and her pride that she could be as wise as God. He first posed a question to her of God's will by asking, **"Has God said?"**

Satan starts deception by putting a thought in a person's mind to question God's will on an area. He creates doubt about it. He says to the mind, "God doesn't really mean it that way." Then, if he goes further, he appeals to a person's pride by saying, "You'll be better off, you will be smarter, you will become fulfilled in your identity, or you will have it all if you will listen and follow through with my thoughts."

Obviously, the deceiver distracted Eve from her partner. Satan pulls people away from those who love them and who can help them discern so he can feed them his thoughts. He attempts to pull believers away from others who can see trouble that they can't see and to withdraw them from that close fellowship.

2

(Note: Many times people have "blind spots" they cannot see. Policemen have said that every driver has a "blind spot" that requires not only looking in the mirrors but turning around to look so as not to pull out into oncoming traffic and cause an accident. Many Christians think they can see everything and sometimes they can't see it all. We all need help from others who've been driving, or walking with Jesus, longer than we have.)

After Eve was deceived, she proceeded to convince her partner that the wrong she was in was "right." If Adam had prayed immediately and listened to his heart, God would have told him differently. Instead, Adam listened to and acted on Eve's deception. Without praying, he knowingly sinned. They both fell into sin and lost their home, their innocence, their carefree life, their dominion in the earth and their continual fellowship with God. Driven with shame into a land they had to work, sweat and cry over, their children became divided. Then the day came when one murdered the other. Cain thought no one would ever know, but you can't hide sin. **"...be sure your sin will find you out"** (Numbers 32:23). Cain was discovered, cast out and marked for the rest of his life *because he would not repent.*

Through Adam and Eve's failure to heed God's instructions, deception and sin entered the earth and have been in the earth throughout time. However, there were those from that first family and

> *"...be sure your sin will find you out" (Numbers 32:23).*

in later generations who chose to walk in fellowship with God and turn from deception. God has always been drawn to help those who choose to listen to Him and obey Him. God loves man and is always reaching out to help anyone who will humbly reach out to receive His help and daily look to Him.

TAKING HEED TO OURSELVES

*T*he Scripture tells us that the deceiver (Satan) is still in the earth today to try to *disqualify* Christians from the race (Revelation 12:9; 1 Peter 5:8-9). One day he'll be cast into the bottomless pit and shut up for a thousand years, no longer able to deceive the nations (Revelation 20:3). He will then be cast into the lake of fire and brimstone forever (Revelation 20:10). But until that time, we, as believers, must learn from the Word of God the enemy's tactics of deception. We can recognize and stop him from disqualifying our lives or the lives of others around us.

Some Christians believe that if they are born again, filled with the Holy Spirit, go to church once a week and know their doctrine of belief, they could never become deceived.

I remember talking to a strong Christian friend once who I had become concerned about. She told me that she spent time in the Word and prayer daily and felt she could never be deceived. My spirit arose within me like an alarm button that had been pushed. I said to her, "Don't ever say that. I also pray daily and believe John 10:4-5 that I hear the Good Shepherd's voice, and the stranger's voice I recognize and do not follow. However, to make a statement that I could never be deceived is moving into the realm of spiritual pride." In fact, Paul said in 1 Corinthians 10:12, **"Wherefore let him that thinketh he standeth take heed lest he fall."** We are to constantly keep a position of "taking heed to ourselves." *We are not to be afraid of the devil or fearful of being*

> *We are not to be afraid of the devil or fearful of being deceived, but we are to keep ourselves in the spirit of meekness and soberness.*

deceived, but we are to keep ourselves in the spirit of meekness and soberness.

Taking heed to yourself is to be alert and on guard, watching for any signs of snares, traps, questionable situations, or wrong attitudes, thoughts and actions in your own life. The more we continue in God's Word, the more we understand and grow in discernment.

For the word of God is quick, and powerful, and sharper than any twoedged sword, piercing even to the dividing asunder of soul and spirit, and of the joints and marrow, and is a discerner of the thoughts and intents of the heart.

Hebrews 4:12

Hosea 4:6 says, **"My people are destroyed for lack of knowledge...."** Many Christians fail to get a knowledge of Scripture to establish what they believe and to strengthen their ability to recognize error. We need to read and study God's Word daily to know right from wrong. But knowledge of God's Word is just the beginning. Wisdom is the ability to rightly apply the knowledge. Understanding can then come as we apply the knowledge. God instructs us in the book of Proverbs to get knowledge, wisdom, understanding and discretion.

He taught me also, and said unto me, Let thine heart retain my words: keep my commandments, and live.

Get wisdom, get understanding: forget it not; neither decline from the words of my mouth.

Proverbs 4:4-5

As we begin to understand our enemy's tactics and we apply God's directives to counter him, we can walk in discretion. In his "Basic Youth Conflict" material, Bill Gothard defines *discretion* as "the ability to avoid thoughts, attitudes and actions that could lead to undesirable consequences."

When wisdom entereth into thine heart, and knowledge is pleasant unto thy soul;

Discretion shall *preserve* [or keep] thee, understanding shall keep thee.

Proverbs 2:10-11

Peter explains to us in 1 Peter 5:8-9:

Be sober [awake], be vigilant [watchful and never off your guard]; because your adversary the devil, as a roaring lion, walketh about, seeking [or searching for any Christian who is off guard and easy to attack] whom he may devour [defeat; swallow up]:

Whom resist stedfast in the faith [and I might add, walking in the God-kind of love], knowing that the same afflictions are accomplished in your brethren that are in the world.

Dr. Lester Sumrall said to us once how it bothered him when people joked about the devil and spoke that he had no power. He went on to say that he wasn't afraid of the devil and knew that Jesus defeated him, but to say that the devil had no power to do anything was deception. If he had no

> *We cannot have a passive attitude that just because we believe and agree with Scripture, we are strong.*

power, why would Scripture tell us he is walking about seeking Christians to devour, and why would we need the whole armor of God to withstand and overcome him (Ephesians 6:10-18)?

We must realize as 1 John 4:4 says, once we are born again, we are of God and have the power within us to overcome Satan and his antichrist or demonic spirits, for **"...greater is he that is in [us], than he that is in the world."** However, it isn't enough to know this. *We must actively enforce this scripture in our lives* and be sober to Satan's subtle devices. We cannot have a *passive* attitude that just because we believe and agree with Scripture, we are strong. Strength that overcomes is watchful in recognizing, confronting and resisting the enemy.

Each believer has weak areas that must be guarded, kept in line with the Word of God and submitted to the Holy Spirit. When we think that we are beyond temptation, we are in a danger zone. I am not saying to focus on weaknesses. We are to focus on God's Word and His overcoming power. However, we are to keep a humble mind before Him. It is by God's grace we are what we are.

Walk with an awareness of the hour we're living in and an awareness of the enemy's tactics. Walk in a sensitivity to the Holy Spirit's voice. Realize the Holy Spirit has been given to us to guide us into all truth (John 16:13). He speaks to us in the still small voice within our hearts as we listen to His gentle promptings and checks. Don't shove His voice aside. Learn to listen. Be sensitive to others around you, especially those who truly love you. Sometimes God speaks to us what we don't want to hear, but if we will wait upon Him and not turn Him away, He will show us what we need to see from a higher perspective. Remember, He loves you! Let His Word and His Holy Spirit daily work His will and purpose in you.

Awake!

Ephesians 5:14 says:

Awake thou that sleepest, and arise from the dead, and Christ shall give thee light.

Paul had just written to the Ephesian church that they were to separate themselves from fornication, uncleanness, covetousness, obscene conversation and perversion and that they were to walk as children of light. Obviously, they were still walking in sinful lifestyles. He compared them to being spiritually asleep and dead, and he told them to awake and rise from the dead.

If you were to put a dead person and a sleeping person next to one another, you would not be able to tell them apart. Christians who are living like others in the world and who don't allow the lordship of Jesus in their lives cannot be distinguished as Christians. They are asleep and look as spiritually dead as those who are spiritually dead.

9

Paul goes on to say, **"See then that ye walk circum-spectly, not as fools, but as wise, redeeming the time, because the days are evil"** (Ephesians 5:15-16). *Dake's Translation* says, "Walk about watching on every hand to avoid danger and enemies — live the gospel by watching your conduct, buying up those moments which others throw away...Be sober."[1]

Paul says in Romans 13:11-14:

And that, knowing the time, that now it is high time to awake out of sleep: for now is our salvation nearer than when we believed.

The night is far spent, the day is at hand: let us therefore cast off the works of darkness, and let us put on the armour of light.

Let us walk honestly, as in the day; not in rioting and drunkenness, not in chambering and wantonness, not in strife and envying.

But put ye on the Lord Jesus Christ, and make not provision for the flesh, to fulfil the lusts thereof.

We are at war spiritually. Our enemy doesn't sleep. God doesn't sleep either. But we must do our part to stay awake and be sober and alert spiritually, *cooperating* with God's wisdom and His delivering help in our lives.

---

[1] Dake, Finis Jennings. *Dake's Annotated Reference Bible*, Lawrenceville, GA: Dake Bible Sales, Inc., 1963, 1991, p. 211.

PRIDE OPENS THE DOOR TO DECEPTION

*H*umility is God's requirement for staying on track and not becoming deceived. Obadiah verse 3 says, **"The pride of thine heart hath deceived thee...."** Pride opens the door to deception.

Pride is an attitude of self-sufficiency. Pride causes a person to feel that they don't need others but are sufficient in their own strength, knowledge, or talents. Satan fell from heaven because he felt he was more than gifted in himself and didn't need God. He also wanted the glory of being the leader and not the assistant.

Pride causes a person to feel so capable of handling life that they don't need to seek God daily for advice. A prideful person is not willing to receive correction because he or she feels that they are okay or they are justified by their actions. Usually, pride makes a person feel that it is others who need to change, not themselves. Someone with pride normally resents correction and speaks against anyone who tries to lovingly bring correction.

A person with too high of an opinion of themselves is usually headed for a humbling experience to pull them down a few notches. Pride will cause a person to reason away their attitudes and actions by justifying themselves so they don't have to change. When challenged, this person cannot face truth because the truth makes him or her

11

look bad. They feel they have to keep up a certain appearance to others, even if they're crumbling apart inside.

If something has gone wrong, when confronted, pride will cause a person to blame others immediately instead of looking inward for any personal fault or failure. When in pride, a person rejects help because of the need to feel in control and self-sufficient to handle everything. Pride causes a person to be insecure and jealous of others who do better. They can't understand why they are not seeing great progress. Yet, they still won't look within to see a need for repentance or change. When we look at King Saul, we see a man who was insecure, yet he felt he must portray himself as stronger than everyone in order to lead them.

Instead of keeping a humble position of obeying God, Saul made decisions based on what he thought and wanted to do. In 1 Samuel 15, when Samuel the prophet had told him God's instructions, he disobeyed and acted on the lust of his flesh. (Note: A godly leader listens to and values godly instruction from others in leadership who listen to God, too.) Samuel confronted Saul's disobedience. Saul quickly lied and blamed the people for his actions, instead of repenting to God and accepting full responsibility.

A deceived person, when caught, will immediately lie to cover his sin and will then blame other people or his circumstances for his course of action. When Saul realized that he would lose his position as king, fearfully he told Samuel not to tell anyone, hoping he could "keep up the act" for a while. (Notice, pride will cause the anointing to lift from someone while they continue to function in their position of leadership, but it will become apparent to all who are looking on.)

In 1 Samuel 28, we see that Saul still wouldn't repent in a true repentance. He went to the witch of Endor (a psychic) to get direction because he couldn't hear from God anymore. Christians who refuse the Holy Spirit's promptings and corrections gradually get where they can't hear the leading of God anymore. Some go from one counselor to another, never fac-

> *Those who are not quick to repent, even over the small things, do not realize they are "dulling" their sensitivity to hear God's voice.*

ing their real problem of going their own way and doing what they want to do. Others seek psychics. Those who seek counsel from psychics open themselves up to the demonic realm. Those who simply go from one counselor to another never face responsibility for their own faults. They do not determine to do what is necessary to correct them, and thus they never move forward in life.

Those who are not quick to repent, even over the small things, do not realize they are *"dulling"* their sensitivity to hear God's voice. They then begin operating in their own reasoning. Sometimes they think they are still able to hear God's voice and they interpret their own desires and thoughts as God's will. However, it will become evident after some time that they are simply living by their own reasoning and not by God's leading.

True Repentance

True repentance is *not just being sorry for getting caught*. True repentance causes a person to grieve that the relationship and fellowship with God are broken. As a result, there is a need to confess and take responsibility for his or her actions.

Paul defines the fruit or evidence of true repentance:

Now I rejoice, not that ye were made sorry, but that ye sorrowed to repentance: for ye were made sorry after a godly manner, that ye might receive damage by us in nothing.

For godly sorrow worketh repentance to salvation not to be repented of: but the sorrow of the world worketh death.

For behold this selfsame thing, that ye sorrowed after a godly sort, what carefulness it wrought in you, yea, what clearing of yourselves, yea, what indignation, yea, what fear, yea, what vehement desire, yea, what zeal, yea, what revenge! In all things ye have approved yourselves to be clear in this matter.

2 Corinthians 7:9-11

Godly sorrow from true repentance produces:

1. A carefulness to avoid traps and any appearance of evil that could entangle you in sin again.

2. A clearing of yourself to want to ensure that others realize there has been a change of behavior and a desire to reconcile with others, if needed.

3. An indignation or hatred of the sin because of the fear of the Lord ruling in your heart (Proverbs 8:14).

4. A vehement desire or zeal to go after God with total commitment, not with half-heartedness or passivity.

5. A revenge to do more for God's Kingdom in order to avenge the devil.

In Matthew 3:8, John the Baptist said to the people,

"Bring forth therefore fruits meet for repentance." In other words, fruit that is evidence of your repentance.

I've noticed through the years that many times Christians want to repent by confessing and asking forgiveness. They expect everyone to forget and accept them on the same terms as

> *The way to rebuild and re-establish trust and closeness is through humility, servanthood and accountability.*

before they sinned, accepting no responsibility for changing behavioral patterns. *Forgiveness should be immediate, because God forgives us immediately when we ask. However, when your sin has hurt other people, there needs to be an effort to correct the harm that was done. There also must be a willingness to allow time to rebuild trust and give others the opportunity to see an attitude of humility, an effort to walk in a new behavior, and an attitude of doing what is best to benefit those who are hurt.*

I've watched some Christians ask forgiveness but not make any effort to rebuild trust and correct things that need to be corrected. This is why others don't trust them and do not want to become close with them again. It is not that they are "holding a grudge." It is a cautious and guarded attitude to keep from being hurt again.

The way to rebuild and re-establish trust and closeness is through *humility, servanthood* and *accountability.* If people see that someone wants to place themselves in an accountable position to others to be kept "in check," then they are willing to trust and allow closeness again. Someone who is unwilling to be accountable cannot be trusted. We all need accountability.

Then there is a hatred or disdain of that sin not to do it again for fear of cutting off relationship with our Father God and with others.

The root cause of incomplete repentance is pride. King Saul lost everything because of his pride.

James 4:6 says, **"...God resisteth the proud, but giveth grace unto the humble."** *God resists the proud because they resist His voice.* Saul would not humble himself, admit his wrong and reveal his need for God. He sought the psychic or witch of Endor. *The "psychic" called forth a familiar spirit (a demon in the disguise of Samuel) to speak to Saul.* We know this was not Samuel because the scripture indicates all those saints who died went to Abraham's bosom and were kept there until Jesus' resurrection. No witch or psychic could call forth any saint of God. *It is beyond their power.* They only have the power of deception to call forth demonic spirits. Jesus was the only One Who could call forth those held in paradise when He descended to the lower parts of the earth and opened the door for them to arise and ascend to heaven (Ephesians 4:8-10).

Let's go back and review the *characteristics* of pride that we have discussed:

Pride...

1. Is self-sufficient. (One reason why many Christians don't take time with God daily to read His Word and pray.)

2. Feels it can get by without others; it is an independent spirit. (Some Christians feel they don't need to go to church. They feel they're the temple of God wherever they are. Some ministries feel they don't need to go to a church. Some churches feel they don't need other churches.)

3. Wants the glory of being the leader, but most of the

16

time can't handle the responsibility. (Note: Jesus told His disciples, **"...he that is greatest among you shall be your servant"** (Matthew 23:11). In other words, if you want to be great in God's Kingdom, learn to serve and accept responsibility. Become faithful to work and serve doing all that's necessary.)

4. Is unable to receive correction and justifies all its actions. Resents others' attempts to correct and instruct. Explains away all actions. Finds it too difficult to say, "I was wrong — forgive me." (Note: It is not repentance to say, "*If* I did anything wrong to hurt you, forgive me." "*If*" proves you are not willing to take responsibility for the wrong. This is "surface level, incomplete repentance." It must be, "I was wrong. Please forgive me.")

5. Feels it is everyone else who is at fault and needs to change, not him or her.

6. Speaks against anyone who tries to lovingly bring corrective help. **"By pride and insolence comes only contention, but with the well-advised is skillful and godly Wisdom"** (Proverbs 13:10 AMP).

7. Has a high opinion of self. **"Pride goes before destruction, and a haughty spirit before a fall"** (Proverbs 16:18 AMP).

8. Can't face truth because it makes him or her look bad, even if crumbling apart on the inside.

9. Can't see "blind spots." (Every Christian must realize there are blind spots that we must seek to see.)

10. Is jealous of others who do well and yet won't look within to see what is blocking them from doing better.

11. Is insecure.

12. Lies when sin is confronted or error is exposed. Is in *denial.*

13. Blames others for failure and won't take any responsibility for it.

14. Tries to go on when anointing has lifted as if everything is still the same. (This applies also to leadership in a marriage and family. Someone who fails at one marriage and still will not admit fault and make changes, but goes ahead into another relationship, will do so with no anointing for leadership.)

15. Does everything for selfish reasons instead of determining what will benefit or be the best for others around them.

16. Repents only because caught, but does not have true repentance which will bring God's mercy and grace.

17. Seeks out other forms of hearing direction since not able to hear from God personally anymore.

18. Will not submit to authority because it feels it is the authority.

Pride feels it knows better than others and cannot be reasoned with. James 3:17 says the wisdom of God is **"...first pure, then peaceable, gentle, and easy to be intreated, full of mercy and good fruits, without partiality, and without hypocrisy."**

I remember a man who had trouble submitting to authority. He put on a false humility around everyone. Outwardly, he acted as if he was a servant of the Lord, but when told what to do and what he could not do, he would always do what he thought instead. It presented problems to the point that assigned leaders had to ask him to stop going with their group. He then found other ministry groups to go out with, but his insubordination never changed. His marriage relationship also suffered because of his lack of subjection in the church and accountability with others.

Later, he felt he was to be a missionary overseas. He came to us wanting to be licensed, ordained and sent forth. Since he had not been submissive to others, our ministry felt we could not license, ordain and send him overseas. He then found a Christian agency that would send him, but it did not check on his relationship within the local church here in the U. S.

When he moved overseas, he was a problem to other missionaries. He divorced his wife and quickly married a younger woman of that country. Immediately he broke away from other Christian ministries to do his own thing. The last we heard of him, he was struggling. Several of us tried to reason with him, but he would not receive our counsel. Regretfully, we've known of others who have taken the same path he took. Pride and lack of submission brought deception and heartache.

How Do We Stop Pride?

Here are some of the ways you can stop pride:

1. You must humble yourself to God and to His *Word*. (God won't humble you, but He'll allow your life to become a humbling setting.) Realize you need Him and *daily* draw to Him (James 4:8; Hebrews 10:22). Instead of living your life your way, surrender daily to the lordship of Jesus and to His will. Our theme song shouldn't be, "I did it my way," but "I surrender all." Daily surrender your

> *Instead of living your life your way, surrender daily to the lordship of Jesus and to His will.*

will to Him. *Submit yourself to Him. Submission* means to adapt yourself and to be willing to yield to Him, not demanding your own way. Submitting to Him also means submitting to His Word. *Your life must be kept in submission to the balance of the whole counsel of the Scriptures, not just the ones you like.*

2. Choose to submit yourself to those who watch over you spiritually and must give account to God for your soul (Hebrews 13:17). If you are in ministry, make sure you are rightly related to another minister(s) or ministry who has the ability to speak into your life.

3. Choose to submit yourself one to another in the Body of Christ in fear of the Lord (Ephesians 5:22). Have a Christian friend, and if you are married, build a good friendship with your spouse whom you can confide in, who will pray for you and help you to see "blind spots" in your life, and vice versa. Don't take offense and break a relationship that could save you spiritually.

4. Be willing to adjust and adapt with other believers around you when you are together. In this way, you will grow in relating to more people as you do your part in the Kingdom.

5. Have a submissive (or adaptable) attitude in your home with your mate as you both have a godly fear of the Lord.

6. If we are going to be wise and have others view us as wise, we would do well to make it our aim to be pure in our motives, peaceable instead of being quick in responding with our emotions, gentle, willing to listen to counsel, full of mercy and good fruits and not hypocritical (James 3:17).

7. Be open to God using other Christians to expand

you or to help you grow in areas you haven't been aware of your need to grow in. Realize God and the Church of Jesus Christ are bigger than "your four and no more" group. Value others around you and their differences, for they each bring variety into the Body of Christ (Philippians 2:3).

8. Be willing to be flexible in areas that do not compromise moral convictions or foundational biblical beliefs.

9. Pray for God to show you how to live your life in your home or around others in such a way that they are benefitted instead of living your life to benefit *yourself*.

Remember that honor will be obtained through humility. **"A man's pride will bring him low, but he who is of a humble spirit will obtain honor"** (Proverbs 29:23 AMP).

4

SELF-DECEIVED

Deception can come from two different channels into our lives. First, deception can come from within when a person becomes self-deceived. James 1:22 says a person who is a hearer of the Word of God but not a doer is *self-deceived.* **"But be ye doers of the word, and not hearers only,** *deceiving your own selves."*

John Wesley, the founder of the Methodist Church, once said that the greatest enemy of the church is "mental assent." In every church, there are believers who mentally agree with and believe the Scriptures. Some can quote their beliefs and even teach them to others, but they are not walking in the whole counsel of truth they believe and teach. Some faithfully come and hear a preacher preach every week and even go to special Christian conferences to be blessed, but they have not brought their lives into subjection to the Word of God to live by it. When the storms come, their house falls because it was built on sand and not on the rock of being a doer of the Word. They have not learned to obey the still small voice of the Holy Spirit Who is trying to lead them. (See Luke 6:46-49.)

I've watched some Christians fall apart in storms of life. *They blame everyone else for their difficulties instead of allowing God to change them* and establish their lives on the rock of doing His Word. I've also watched the *same* storms come against other Christians and they stood strong and went forward. Doing the Word isn't always easy and doesn't receive the attention that we'd like to have for doing it, but it reaps long-lasting fruit.

> *Four factors that feed self-deception are apathy, pride, selfishness and continual disobedience.*

Four factors that feed self-deception are *apathy, pride, selfishness* and *continual disobedience*:

1. *Apathy* - Webster defines *apathy* as "lack of emotion, lack of interest and indifference."[1] Apathy can set into a person who feels they've worked hard to grow and now they can "coast" awhile. They become complacent. They continue coming to church out of habit but have no desire to press into God anymore. When someone is not seeking to grow, they are backsliding and losing what they've received.

2. *Pride* - Webster's definition of *pride* to which I am referring is "excessive self-esteem and conceit."[2] Usually pride occurs when a person feels they have acquired enough knowledge of the Word that they can handle life without seeking God daily in the Word. They think they are too busy and begin to feel that they're making good decisions and are talented enough to do well on their own.

---

[1] *Webster's II New Riverside Dictionary*, Boston, MA: Houghton Mifflin Co., 1984, p. 34.
[2] Ibid., p. 555.

3. *Selfishness* - Webster's definition of *selfishness* to which I am referring is "self-centered and self-seeking."[3] It is "acting for or thinking of one's own well-being alone."[4] Selfishness gradually comes back after a Christian has settled into their walk with Jesus. Every Christian must purpose to overcome selfishness daily. Some, however, observe others who have or do things that are like the world and are socially accepted. They feel justified that they should be able to do whatever they want to do. The problem is that they forget Who it is that they should be trying to please. They are pleasing themselves while Jesus stands at the door of their heart knocking.

As Christians we must stop and ask ourselves on a regular basis, "Who am I seeking to please?" The answer should be, *God and others.* First Thessalonians 4:1 NASB says, **"Finally then, brethren, we request and exhort you in the Lord Jesus, that, as you received from us instruction as to how you ought to walk and please God (just as you actually do walk), that you may excel still more."** Philippians 2:3-4 NASB says, **"Do nothing from selfishness or empty conceit, but with humility of mind let each of you** *regard one another as more important than himself; do not merely look out for your own personal interests, but also for the interests of others."*

Over the years, I've watched as some Christians have broken off relationships from others because of selfishness. I've seen it in marriage relationships being torn apart, and I've seen it in people leaving churches over their

---

[3] Ibid., p. 628.
[4] *Webster's 21st Century Dictionary*, Nashville, TN: Thomas Nelson, Publishers, 1993, p. 237.

own selfish ways. A selfish person will be critical of others and will not see their own self-centered ways. They will never find genuine and consistent joy and peace because they have not allowed Jesus (the selfless One) to rule their lives. A self-centered Christian will ultimately become lukewarm spiritually.

In Revelation 3:15-22 Jesus said:

I know thy works, that thou art neither cold nor hot: I would thou wert cold or hot.

So then because thou art *lukewarm, and neither cold nor hot, I will spue thee out of my mouth.*

Because thou sayest, I am rich, and increased with goods, and have need of nothing; and knowest not that thou art wretched, and miserable, and poor, and blind, and naked:

I counsel thee to buy of me gold tried in the fire, that thou mayest be rich; and white raiment, that thou mayest be clothed, and that the shame of thy nakedness do not appear; and anoint thine eyes with eyesalve, that thou mayest see.

As many as I love, I rebuke and chasten: be zealous therefore, and repent.

Behold, *I stand at the door, and knock: if any man hear my voice, and open the door, I will come in to him, and will sup* [fellowship] *with him, and he with me.*

To him that overcometh will I grant to sit with me in my throne, even as I also overcame, and am set down with my Father in his throne.

He that hath an ear, let him hear what the Spirit saith unto the churches.

26

I remember the day we came out of church services and someone met us with the news that a pastor and his wife, whom we knew personally, had just announced their plans to divorce. It hit me so hard, I literally wept right at that moment, and cried out, "Oh, Jesus, no." Then I found myself praying in the Holy Spirit prayer language, asking the Lord Jesus to intervene.

We called them and went to speak with them. We listened to them individually, asking why and if there was a way they could reconcile. We grieved for their family as well as for their church and for others who knew them.

The reason for divorce was not abuse or immorality, but because the husband was no longer happy. He made the statement, "I'm going to find someone to be happy with. I've been unhappy so long, and I feel I deserve to be happy." What a deception! He married within a few months, but ended that marriage within one year.

Friend, no person can make you happy. You can get a moment of counterfeit happiness, but it will leave quickly. Jesus is the only One Who can give you happiness and satisfy the longing that's in your soul. He can only satisfy it when you are willing to humble yourself and hunger and thirst for Him. Then you'll be willing to "lose your life for His sake so you can save it" (Luke 9:24-25).

I could give you story after story of how this *selfish* way of thinking has hurt and ruined the lives of many Christians. Selfishness is a very prevalent attitude in our world system. I remember my husband sharing a message entitled, "What's In It for Me?" Those who are self-centered only do what benefits their own personal interests. If it requires them to give up something for someone else's benefit, immediately they say, "I don't feel led to do that," or, "You make me feel bad or uncomfortable."

Could it be the reason they are uncomfortable is that they are convicted by the Holy Spirit to change and they are stubbornly resisting His voice? If they do a good deed, they first check and see what it will do for them. Will it make them look good in the eyes of others? Will it bring promotion for them? Will they be able to get a return of favor from whomever they favor? Will it make them feel good? All of these reasons are centered around "self."

Jesus didn't say, "Follow Me and I'll make you happy." He said:

> **"Anyone who wants to follow me must put aside his own desires and conveniences and carry his cross with him every day and keep close to me! Whoever loses his life for my sake will save it, but whoever insists on keeping his life will lose it; and what profit is there in gaining the whole world when it means forfeiting one's self?"**
>
> **Luke 9:23-25** TLB

The *King James Version* of verse 25 says, **"For what is a man advantaged, if he gain the whole world, and lose himself, or be cast away?"** To be *cast away* means "to be cast out or off; to be shipwrecked, thrown away, or discarded; to be cast adrift or stranded, as by shipwreck."[5] What advantage is it for a Christian to go after things in this world system and become shipwrecked spiritually?

This is why Romans 12:1-2 says we are to present

---

[5] *Webster's New World Dictionary*, Second College Edition, New York, NY: Simon & Schuster, 1982, p. 221.

our lives unto God daily as a living sacrifice. Be willing to sacrifice your will and desires for His will and desires. Be willing to adjust yourself so others around you are not always having to adjust to your selfishness. Then in verse 2 Paul says we must not become conformed to this present world system (or attitudes of the world around us) but become transformed as we renew our minds daily with His Word.

You are not a "Word" person or a "Spirit-filled" person if you are walking by the dictates of your flesh and not making the effort to bring your flesh under submission to God's Word. We all have to bring our flesh under subjection to the Spirit of God daily. However, some people don't even try to bring their flesh under. Instead, they make excuses for it and laugh or shrug off any conviction about it. I've watched this attitude lead Christians to hardship, broken relationships and hurts which could have been avoided had they listened to God's voice. I've also seen selfishness so take over some lives that it led to their death.

Proverbs 18:1 TLB says, **"The selfish man quarrels against every sound principle of conduct by demanding his own way."**

Self-deception is hard for a person to see if they won't allow others to speak into their life and stay in a position of accountability to someone.

Remember how King Saul resisted the sound principle that God had spoken to him through Samuel and went his own way? He lost his position as king and the anointing of God that had been upon him. Ultimately, he lost his life and his son's life. Most of all, he lost his relationship with God.

Selfishness isn't worth the price a person pays for it.

4. *Continual Disobedience* - A person who willfully continues in disobedience in an area will become deceived. Often, they offer a small sacrifice to make up for the disobedience. King Saul thought he could offer a sacrifice of some sheep to God to cover his disobedience. Samuel confronted him, and then said that God desires obedience and not sacrifice (1 Samuel 15:22). A sacrifice cannot cover or remove disobedience. Disobedience must be repented of, followed by a change in the person's lifestyle.

> *Self-deception is hard for a person to see if they won't allow others to speak into their life and stay in a position of accountability to someone.*

Self-deception can happen when a Christian is a doer of the Word of God in one area but resists doing the Word in another area, then blames God for all the promises not working for them.

For example, I've known of people who began to tithe and give offerings, believing Malachi 3:10 that the devil would be rebuked and the windows of heaven would be opened to them. However, they would not stop their compulsive behavior patterns. Some would not remove immoral TV, videos and literature. They wondered why they did not have enough money to pay their bills or for other needs.

I've known of some singles who have had sexual involvement on a regular basis and still went to church and tithed, thinking they were okay. Some have quoted scriptures to me and shared their belief in Malachi 3:10, then said, "I don't know why it isn't working."

I've seen people who've not brought their anger and strife under control. They wondered why God did not bless their lives because they were giving into the Kingdom. If you are *knowingly* violating a commandment of God in one area and obeying His command in another, don't expect God to bless the double standard.

I remember a Christian who was very quick tempered and could explode on his family members or church friends at any situation that didn't go to his liking. He wouldn't recognize his sin of "lack of self-control." Sad to say, he felt God didn't keep His Word when he didn't prosper for his giving.

Friend, God watches over His Word to perform it (Jeremiah 1:12). *We* stop the promises of God by our lack of submission to the whole counsel of God's Word.

> *If you are knowingly violating a commandment of God in one area and obeying His command in another, don't expect God to bless the double standard.*

Another Christian who started tithing came to us one day and asked us why they weren't being blessed. I found out they weren't working and thought they were living by faith. Living by faith doesn't mean not working. No matter what job you work at, you will need to live by faith in God, because things of this world change and our trust must be in God as our Source.

The Word of God says, **"...if any would not work, neither should he eat"** (2 Thessalonians 3:10). First Timothy 5:8 says, **"But if any provide not for his own,** and **specially for those of his own house,** *he hath denied the faith,* **and is worse than an infidel."** Those who don't work and say they're living by faith are actually denying the faith that God's Word teaches. Giving a boss a good day's work without complaining and criticizing will attract God's blessings to come your way.

James 1:22 says, **"But be ye doers of the word, and not hearers only,** *deceiving your own selves."* A person who is just a hearer of God's Word is one who comes to church, hears the Word, maybe even participates in a daily Bible reading plan, but is looking into the mirror and walking away, forgetting what he or she saw. This person is like a man beholding his natural face in a glass or in a mirror. He sees his need and he sees what needs to be changed, but he goes his way and forgets what he saw (James 1:23-25). He makes no effort to change and adjust his life or submit to the lordship of the Word of God.

Some people come to church. They hear the Word of God preached on how to live their life in Jesus Christ and how to walk with Jesus. After church, they go away saying, "That was a good message." By the weekend they are out with someone having a sexual relationship, lying, or cheating, following their own selfish desires and ignoring God's voice. Without thinking, they are breaking their covenant with God. These people are deceiving themselves. Our covenant with God is a two-way commitment. God's covenant promises have conditions to be followed if we are to receive His covenant benefits.

5

THE DECEITFULNESS OF SIN

*T*here has been a thought that when someone accepts Christ as a child, no matter if they live like the devil the rest of their life, they are saved. When they die they will go to heaven. This thought does not line up with Scripture. It's time for Christians to live as new creations and as evident disciples of Jesus.

Remember, Jesus said:

And because iniquity shall abound, the love of many shall wax cold.

***But* he that shall *endure* unto the end, the same shall be saved.**

Matthew 24:12-13

Our love for Jesus is supposed to endure until the end. The Gospel is not a Gospel of convenience but of *commitment*.

I'm amazed at people who believe that once they got saved when they were a child, they are always saved and can live any way they want to. If this is true, then every Christian should feel free to live a life of sin to the "max" so they can experience all the world has to offer before

> *The Gospel is not a Gospel of convenience but of commitment.*

going to heaven.

Paul wrote to the Romans in chapter 6, verses 1 and 2:

...Shall we continue in sin, that grace may abound?

God forbid. How shall we, that are dead to sin, live any longer therein?

Our desire should be as one minister said, "Once we accept Jesus in our hearts, we walk in the door, stay behind the door, under the blood of the doorpost and don't come out." That is where our safety and our eternal security are, but it is a daily choice to stay surrendered and submitted to His lordship.

I'm not planning on getting out of Jesus. I'm planning on staying in Him and abiding in Him the rest of my life on this earth and being with Him in heaven. There are some who've been deceived, thinking that they could live in any lifestyle they choose and not suffer any consequences.

> *Sin is deceitful because it makes a person think they can get away with their disobedience when they don't see an immediate penalty for it.*

Basically, sin is man going his own way rather than obeying the voice of God speaking in his heart. Sin causes a person to do what self wants rather than what God desires. Jesus came to redeem us from going our own way (Isaiah 53:5).

Sin is deceitful because it makes a person think they can get away with their disobedience when they don't see an immediate penalty for it.

I remember seeing a Christian friend who I had not

seen in awhile. I asked how she was doing. A year earlier I had prayed with her regarding her marriage. Her husband had left her for another person at work. They had been in the ministry a few years earlier but had left the ministry because of offense. He had attended church services some but was not consistent. He started

> *Agape love is the God-kind of love. It is unconditional and loves in spite of circumstances or in spite of how the other person reciprocates.*

working on Sundays in order to have an excuse to tell people he could not come to church anymore.

With no spiritual influence around him, he was no longer convicted of sin, so it was easier to go ahead with an affair. He simply shoved aside the still small voice of the Holy Spirit and did whatever he wanted to do. It was easy then to say to his wife, "I don't love you anymore." The reason it was easy was because he did not have to choose to love her with agape love and lay his life down for her anymore. He left the love of God in order to embrace the sensual, erotic, physical love that is self-seeking and conditional.

Let me briefly explain. Agape love is the God-kind of love. It is unconditional and loves in spite of circumstances or in spite of how the other person reciprocates. It is giving and does what benefits the other person. Jesus exemplified this kind of love for us. He loved us in spite of everything. He went through death on the cross for you and me. He forgave the ones crucifying Him and even prayed for God the Father to forgive them. He said, **"Father, forgive them, for they do not know what they**

are doing" (Luke 23:34 NIV).

Looking at the whole scenario, I would say that the ones who crucified Him knew exactly what they were doing. However, He knew that they didn't know that the devil was manipulating them to crucify Him.

> *I'm glad Jesus didn't bail out on us!*

That is why He said they didn't know what they were doing.

It is truly forgiveness when we not only say we forgive, but we pray for God the Father to forgive those who have hurt or offended us even if we feel they knew what they were doing. Actually, they don't realize they are being controlled by the devil.

Phileo love is a friendship, human type of love. It will cause a person to risk their life for someone they are fond of. The problem occurs, however, when a person stops being fond of another person. It can easily turn to resentment. This kind of love is also conditional.

Then, there is *eros* love, which is a sensual love based on the five physical senses. If someone makes you feel good or if they are pretty or handsome, then there is a love for them. This love is self-centered and seeks to gratify itself. When self is no longer gratified, then this love ends. It is based on whatever benefits oneself. This is why there are so many divorces today. *Eros* love was the foundation of many of these marriages. Once the physical attraction left or the person no longer met their needs, they bailed out. I'm glad Jesus didn't bail out on us!

People who go from one sexual relationship to another will never find fulfillment. You can't find fulfillment in a person. Only Jesus can fulfill you. Once you accept this and go after Him with all your heart, then when you do meet someone who is also going after Jesus, you will love them unconditionally like He loves us.

My friend said to me, "Well, the divorce is now final. He is going to marry the lady he has been living with." She said, "Several Christians have told me that I must accept the fact that he is going to heaven anyway, but that he will just not have any rewards once he gets there." She asked, "Sharon, do you believe that?" I replied, "If he repents and turns from his sin, yes, he will go to heaven. However, if he continues with this other lady, both he and she will go to hell because they are adulterers."

Scripture says adulterers will not inherit the Kingdom of God (Galatians 5:19-21; 1 Corinthians 6:9-10). Proverbs 7:6-27 talks of the adulterous woman who brought down many men and that her house is the way to hell, going down to the chambers of death. Proverbs 6:32 says, **"But whoso committeth adultery with a woman lacketh understanding: he that doeth it destroyeth his own soul."**

Not long ago, I heard the testimony of a person who had allowed her disappointment in her husband to gradually turn her heart away from him. She also allowed the spirit of offense to turn her away from the church where she and her family had attended. She began to be drawn toward another man. First it was an emotional attraction because this man gave her a listening ear, but it developed into a physical relationship. She told her husband she was leaving him and was getting a divorce. She felt justified by her actions. She still read her Bible daily and went to another church once a week where no one knew her.

She told her husband, "God still loves me, no matter

what." Yes, He loves us no matter what, but He is bound from our lives by our choices and actions that are contrary to His will. Their small children didn't understand why their mom had left them. Her husband prayed and stood on God's Word for the salvation of his marriage. Several other people were also praying for her.

One day she read in her Bible from Galatians 5:19-21 that adulterers would not inherit the Kingdom of God. Immediately, the fear of God came upon her and she repented. She returned to her husband and family. A person at church prophesied to her that a relationship she had been in was going to be severed. The person giving the prophecy said he saw an angel with a sword cutting a cord between her and another person.

After that word, the man she had been involved with never contacted her again. It was as if he disappeared from her life. She never made any effort to contact him either. (Note: It is important not to contact someone you've been wrongfully involved with, whether by phone, letter, or in person. No contact sends a loud message: *It's over!* To contact someone you've been involved with in an adulterous situation will cause you to be drawn back into that relationship. Just leave it and cleave to your spouse and to Jesus.)

This lady saw her deception and turned from it. Her family has been redeemed out of the hand of the enemy.

God will always love every human being, but He hates sin. He has given every person a free will to choose life or death, heaven or hell. He will love a person even though they choose to go to hell. But the person who willfully chooses a life of sin and will not repent of it will suffer the consequences of sin. Hell is like a prison.

Someone who continues in crime goes to prison. Prison is to keep people who choose to do wrong and go against the law from continuing to hurt those who want to do right and keep the law.

I asked the friend whose divorce had been finalized legally, "Is your husband going to church anywhere?" She said, "No, it makes him uncomfortable." Wonder why? First John 1:6-7 says:

If we say that we have fellowship with him, and walk in darkness, we lie, and do not the truth:

But if we walk in the light, as he is in the light, we have fellowship one with another, and the blood of Jesus Christ his Son cleanseth us from all sin.

First John 2:4-6 TLB says:

Someone may say, "I am a Christian; I am on my way to heaven; I belong to Christ." But if he doesn't do what Christ tells him to, he is a liar. But those who do what Christ tells them to will learn to love God more and more. That is the way to know whether or not you are a Christian. Anyone who says he is a Christian should live as Christ did.

John 3:19-21 TLB says:

Their sentence is based on this fact: that the Light from heaven came into the world, but *they loved the darkness more than the Light, for their deeds were evil. They hated the heavenly Light because they wanted to sin in the darkness. They stayed away from that Light for fear their sins would be exposed and they would be* *punished.* **But those doing right come gladly to the Light to let everyone see that they are doing what God wants them to.**

If you disagree with what I've written, please read the scriptures and let God speak to your heart. I love people and I will continue to believe God for people who have gone away from Him to change and return to their first love. However, it grieves me to hear Christians apathetically say that it doesn't matter how someone lives. WAKE UP!

Sodom and Gomorrah thought they were okay, too. Even Lot's own family members chose sin instead of obeying the warning of God and taking the opportunity to leave and escape judgment. Sin *does* have its own judgment. Romans 6:23 says, **"For the wages of sin is death; but the gift of God is eternal life through Jesus Christ our Lord."**

Galatians 6:7-9 TLB says:

> **Don't be misled** [*The King James Version* says, **"Be not deceived"**]; **remember that you can't ignore God and get away with it: a man will always reap just the kind of crop he sows! If he sows to please his own wrong desires, he will be planting seeds of evil and he will surely reap a harvest of spiritual decay and death; but if he plants the good things of the Spirit, he will reap the everlasting life which the Holy Spirit gives him. And let us not get tired of doing what is right, for after a while we will reap a harvest of blessing if we don't get discouraged and give up.**

Many people don't realize if they begin a relationship in adultery and unfaithfulness, they will ultimately reap that very situation from the person they are with or from other persons. God's Word is true. Whatever we sow, ultimately we will reap. The way we treat others will come back to us. Whatever choices we make will produce a harvest of blessing or of cursing in our lives. Whatever good things we put into our lives will produce after its kind. Whatever bad things we put into our lives will produce after its kind. The good produces good things, such as love, joy, peace, stability, etc. The bad produces bad things, such as heartache, pain, suffering, confusion, guilt, instability, etc.

Notice, Galatians 6:8-9 says not to get weary of sowing the good things of the Spirit or doing what is right, because you will reap a harvest of God's blessings. Praise God! If you haven't experienced blessings, check your life. Are you sowing good things? If so, keep at it. It will come back to you. God is faithful to His promises (Hebrews 10:23; 2 Corinthians 1:20).

Deception is "being misled to believe an untruth." When someone is deceived into thinking that they're going to make it to heaven no matter how they're living, then God cannot deal with them. He may try to warn or correct, but His still small voice will be shoved aside. Sin hardens the heart to the point a person can't hear (or won't listen to) the voice of God.

> *Whatever we sow, ultimately we will reap. The way we treat others will come back to us.*

41

Hebrews 3:7-8,13 says:

...To day if ye will hear his voice, harden not your hearts...But exhort one another daily, while it is called To day; lest any of you be hardened through the deceitfulness of sin.

Sin's spiritual hardening can be compared to the physical heart's arteries becoming hardened, resulting in a constriction of the blood flow. Sin stops the flow of God's Spirit in a person's life and stops up the channel of our hearing the voice of God.

Sin always looks inviting and appears to be okay. The devil will always try to convince a person that other people are doing the same thing, and they are good people! Sin or disobedience to God creates a sense of independence: "I know what I'm doing and I can handle things." Remember, once you start shoving aside the *still small voice within you,* you can't discern situations and people properly. You begin to make wrong choices and confused judgment of things. This starts a cycle of momentary pleasure, ending in emptiness and a constant struggle to achieve, with no lasting satisfaction.

Sin always requires a payment. Wrong choices end up creating problems and heartache. Those who don't stop and repent from going their own way will end up destroying themselves.

When Christians say, "I can't hear God speak," they should check within their hearts and ask themselves, "Is something not right inside that's causing me not to hear the voice of God?" It's definitely not a problem on God's end of the communication line. I believe that there are reasons why people can't hear God's voice. I believe sometimes God speaks to people to do something and they don't do it because of holding strife, fear, apathy, selfishness, or pride in their hearts. They think that they can just go on the way they're going and still hear God. God expects us to grow and get past being a child that everyone has to cater to. He's calling believers to step up and take the responsibility to obey Him.

Another thought to consider regarding hearing God's voice is, why would God tell someone anything else to do if they're not doing what He already told them to do? Hearing the voice of God takes follow-through of little directives if you intend to hear Him speak in major directional leading at other times in your life.

Deception comes through doing what we want to do instead of what God wants. I've watched many Christians, who profess that Jesus is their Lord, act as if they are their own lord. They develop a lifestyle of doing what they feel like doing, and if they don't feel like it or it doesn't benefit them personally, then they don't do it. When someone lives selfishly they are deceived. A person who is submitted to the lordship of Jesus will look at how others can be benefitted.

Covetousness Can Deceive

At other times, I have seen people covet or want something so much that they deceive themselves into thinking that God has told them that they are going to do or have whatever it is they are coveting. I've had ladies tell me that they've been prophesied to that they were going to marry a particular minister. Some have made preparations for the marriage when the minister they desired to marry had no intention to ever go out with them. The sad result was, when the minister married someone else, they fell apart emotionally. They had been deceived.

I know of a man who, while in seminary, became close friends with three ladies his age. They all loved God and were in classes together. They prayed together and went to church together. They became a very close group, and there was a real flow of the Spirit among them.

The young man was nice looking, caring and very compassionate with people. He was very good at counseling because of being a good listener and being so merciful. His eyes were especially compassionate towards people when he talked with them.

Obviously, those compassionate eyes were misinterpreted. At graduation time, all three of these ladies came up to him at different times and said, "You know, I feel in my spirit that God has called us to be together for the rest of our lives." None of the three knew that the others were doing this. This man was overwhelmed and said, "Well, God hasn't spoken to me about it, but I appreciate you sharing this with me."

He told me, "I knew all along it wasn't any of the three I was called to be with the rest of my life." He ended up marrying a girl from back home that he had known.

How could all three girls feel that God had spoken to them that they were to marry him? Each coveted or desired something by her own flesh so much that appeared to be so obvious, but God didn't speak it.

Through the years, I've had many ladies come to me for prayer regarding a particular man that they have been "told by God" they are going to marry. Some even had prophecies spoken to them regarding it. God speaks to people at times within their heart that they are going to do something or be with someone in ministry, but He never violates the will of a person to force them to marry someone they do not want to marry.

When my husband and I began dating, he had an "open vision" of the two of us together before crowds of people. He didn't tell me this until a year later. I was drawn to him in a different way than I had been with other guys. I had hopes that the relationship would continue, and it did.

When God leads two people together, they will both know it. Through the years, I've instructed the ladies who have come to me to seek first the Kingdom of God and His righteousness. Then I encourage them to allow God to *add* the husband who is best for their lives. As they pray Matthew 6:10 that God's will be done in their lives, God will honor that prayer. We must trust that God wants the best for us and knows the best person for our lives.

Covetousness can deceive. How do you avoid covetousness? Check your motives. Is this desire for your selfish benefit or for the benefit of others? Will this bless the other person? Will this relationship bless other people? If you are desiring a relationship, ask yourself, "Am I willing to release the person I have in mind so Jesus can be my first love? Do I trust God enough that if He leads me apart from this person that He will either lead us back together at another time, or He will bring other people into our lives who are better suited for each of us?" Trust is believing that God wants the *best* for you as much as you do.

God loves us, and He is also jealous for our hearts.

He won't allow a person to take that first place in our hearts. If we pursue our own covetousness, we'll be hurt or disappointed in the end. Pursue Him and He will bring the person into your life who will love you unconditionally and build you up as you do the same for them.

Right Thinking Can Deliver You, But Wrong Thinking Can Destroy You

It seems that in our society today, there's a lot of people calling right wrong and wrong right, especially in this nation. (See Malachi 2:17.) Ephesians 5:6 says, **"Let no man deceive you with vain words...."** They don't know what they're saying. Line up what you hear with what the Word of God says.

Although you may know a single person who is a Christian and they see nothing wrong with sexual intimacy outside of marriage, that doesn't make it right. In fact, the Bible says fornicators will not inherit the Kingdom of God (1 Corinthians 5:9-11).

Society accepts homosexual churches, but that doesn't mean homosexuality is condoned or approved by God.

We must also realize that just because some Christians divorce because they tire of their spouse and lust for someone more attractive, does not bring God's favor and blessing on that next relationship. No matter how many success principles that person operates in, they won't succeed as long as *lust* is driving their life. The church is to accept and forgive people from all walks of life but some have accepted sinful lifestyles, thinking, "God is love, and He turns His face and doesn't notice or judge sin."

This may be a rude awakening, but as I shared earlier, unrepented sin has its own judgment and penalty. It's like gravity. If a man jumps from a sixty-floor building, he'll kill himself. The building and the ground didn't kill him, but he went against a known principle and he killed himself.

> *God calls us to a standard of life that sets us apart from the world's lifestyles.*

God calls us to a standard of life that sets us apart from the world's lifestyles. He then exhorts us to lovingly confront and bring accountability into our lives (1 Thessalonians 5:14; 2 Timothy 2:25-26).

Ye therefore, beloved, seeing ye know these things before, beware lest ye also, being led away with the error of the wicked, fall from your own stedfastness.

2 Peter 3:17

Your body is the temple of God, and you are in covenant relationship with Him. Don't play around with sin. Don't see how close you can get to the edge of it. **"Abstain from all appearance of evil** [or that which would create an opportunity for sin]**"** (1 Thessalonians 5:22). Second Timothy 2:22 TLB says, **"Run from anything that gives you the evil thoughts that young men often have, but stay close to anything that makes you want to do right. Have faith and love, and enjoy the companionship of those who love the Lord and have pure hearts."**

For example, if you are a man and you pass a lingerie store as you are walking in a mall, don't stand there gazing at the dummy who is dressed skimpy. Or, for another example, if you are working with a person who is trying to flirt with you and you are married, change jobs. Get away from tempting situations. Your salvation and your family (if you are married) are worth more than the big money you could make there.

Be Cautious of the Sphere You Live In and the Influence of Others Around You

Guard your close associations! First Corinthians 15:33 says, **"Do not be deceived: 'Bad company corrupts good morals'"** (NASB). You'll eventually become like those you closely associate with. Verse 34 goes on to say, **"Awake to righteousness** [wake up to consciously living right and godly], **and sin not; for some have not the knowledge of God: I speak this to your shame."**

I remember a young Christian woman who worked at a restaurant/bar for a long period of time where she became involved in some relationships that caused her to slowly go down morally. She quit church because she felt awkward. (See 1 John 1:6-7.) Later, she returned to the Lord in repentance and left her job in faith believing for another job. God provided another job, and she is living a redeemed life today.

> *First Corinthians 15:33 says, "Do not be deceived: 'Bad company corrupts good morals'"* (NASB).

You may say, "How can I witness to people if I'm not around them?" Witnessing and close companionship are two different things. Jesus was around sinners and believers, but His close associates were those who were willing to leave all to follow Him. He exemplified a consecrated life to God both publicly and privately. He ate a meal at times with sinners to speak into their lives. He wasn't afraid of talking to them, but His close companions were those who were willing to forsake all and follow Him.

We are called to love, accept and forgive *all* people, but also to bring them into conformity to God's Word through discipleship.

We must lovingly identify sin and help people see that those who continue in sin, who do not repent and turn from it, will not inherit the Kingdom of God. They will not go to heaven when they die if they are living in sin and not making any effort to turn from it. Even if they have received Jesus at one time in their lives but willfully have walked away to live life the way they want to, they will not make it to heaven. The only way they will make heaven is through repentance.

First Corinthians 6:9-10 says, **"Know ye not that the unrighteous shall not inherit the kingdom of God? Be not deceived: neither** *fornicators,* **nor** *idolaters,* **nor** *adulterers,* **nor** *effeminate,* **nor** *abusers of themselves with mankind,* **nor** *thieves,* **nor** *covetous,* **nor** *drunkards,* **nor** *revilers,* **nor** *extortioners,* **shall inherit the kingdom of God."**

Dake's Bible Translation defines *idolatry* as "anything on which affections are passionately set; having an extravagant admiration of the heart for something or someone." *Dake's Translation* calls the *adulterer* "the unfaithful," those involved in "unlawful sexual relations between men and women, single or married." Dake gives the same definition for *fornication* as he does for *adultery,* then adds, "Besides all manner of other unlawful relations." (Perverted sexual acts come under this category — whether within or outside of a marriage relationship.) He defines *thieves* as "robbers"; *covetous* as "the lustful"; *drunkards* as "drinkers of intoxicants"; *revilers* as "abusers of others"; and *extortioners* as "those who obtain by violence or threats." (This would mean physically abusive people will not inherit the Kingdom of God or go to heaven.) Dake says that the *effeminate* are "men who have womanlike traits to an inappropriate degree, wanting in manly strength or aggressiveness; especially marked with weakness, softness and love of ease; over-emotional, or over-delicate...." Those who are *"abusers of themselves with mankind"* are those who submit their bodies to "unnatural lewdness, homosexuality or sexual perversion."[1]

Romans 1:18-32 NASB says:

For the wrath of God is revealed from heaven against all ungodliness and unrighteousness of men, who suppress the truth in unrighteousness,

Because that which is known about God is evident within them; for God made it evident to them.

For since the creation of the world His invisible attributes, His eternal power and divine nature, have been clearly seen, being under-

[1] Dake, Finis Jennings. *Dake's Annotated Reference Bible*, Lawrenceville, GA: Dake Bible Sales, Inc., 1963, 1991, pp. 179,207.

stood through what has been made, so that they are without excuse.

For even though they knew God, they did not honor Him as God, or give thanks; but they became futile in their speculations, and their foolish heart was darkened.

Professing to be wise, they became fools,

And exchanged the glory of the incorruptible God for an image in the form of corruptible man and of birds and four-footed animals and crawling creatures.

Therefore God gave them over in the lusts of their hearts to impurity, that their bodies might be dishonored among them.

For they exchanged the truth of God for a lie, and worshiped and served the creature rather than the Creator, who is blessed forever. Amen.

For this reason God gave them over to degrading passions; for their women exchanged the natural function for that which is unnatural,

And in the same way also the men abandoned the natural function of the woman and burned in their desire toward one another, men with men committing indecent acts and receiving in their own persons the due penalty of their error.

And just as they did not see fit to acknowledge God any longer, God gave them over to a depraved mind, to do those things which are not proper,

Being filled with all unrighteousness, wickedness, greed, evil; full of envy, murder, strife,

deceit, malice; they are gossips,

Slanderers, haters of God, insolent, arrogant, boastful, inventors of evil, disobedient to parents,

Without understanding, untrustworthy, unloving, unmerciful;

And, although they know the ordinance of God, that those who practice such things are worthy of death, they not only do the same, but also give hearty approval to those who practice them.

Paul went on to say in 1 Corinthians 6:11, **"And such were some of you: but ye are washed, but ye are sanctified, but ye are justified in the name of the Lord Jesus, and by the Spirit of our God."** In other words, people come to Jesus from all kinds of backgrounds of sin, but once they receive Him as Lord and Savior, His blood cleanses them from sin and He calls them to walk in a newness of life. Thank God for His mercy and saving grace! Thank God for the ability to walk in a newness of life! He is now inside of you to help you work out your salvation (Philippians 2:12).

First Corinthians 6:19-20 says:

What? know ye not that your body is the temple of the Holy Ghost which is in you, which ye have of God, and ye are not your own?

For ye are bought with a price: therefore glorify God in your body, and in your spirit, which are God's.

Second Corinthians 6:14-17 says:

Be ye not unequally yoked together with unbelievers: for what fellowship hath right-

eousness with unrighteousness? and what communion hath light with darkness?

And what concord hath Christ with Belial? or what part hath he that believeth with an infidel?

And what agreement hath the temple of God with idols? for ye are the temple of the living God; as God hath said, I will dwell in them, and walk in them; and I will be their God, and they shall be my people.

Wherefore *come out from among them, and be ye separate*, saith the Lord, and touch not the unclean thing; and I will receive you.

Your body is the temple of the Holy Spirit, and you are to glorify God with your *body* and with your *spirit*. Some have thought they could live in homosexuality, adultery, incest, abusive anger, strife, cheating, gossiping, lying, etc. and still go to heaven because someone told them it doesn't matter because God loves them anyway. God does love us regardless, but He has given us the will to choose. He allows us to choose to go to heaven or hell by the choices we make while living on the earth. He gives us mercy to repent, to run from and avoid the appearance or opportunity for sin. If you're living in sin, you can repent and surrender to the lordship of Jesus today. You don't have to continue in deception.

> *Your body is the temple of the Holy Spirit, and you are to glorify God with your body and with your spirit.*

Proverbs 28:13 says, **"He that covereth his sins shall not prosper: but whoso confesseth and forsaketh them shall have mercy."** Galatians 6:7 says, **"Be not deceived; God is not mocked: for whatsoever a man soweth, that shall he also reap."** The warning of this is, "Don't go against God's commands or His voice speaking to your heart, or you'll pay for it." The mercy of God is that if you repent of sin, there is not only forgiveness but redemption from your failures and restoration from God as you believe Him. *Sow to righteousness and reap His mercy.*

Over the years, I've seen some who have come to the Lord and repented of sin, *but did not stay in a guarded position.* They began to be pulled back into a sin and thought they could hide it. Ultimately, it was revealed because sin cannot hide too long without negatively affecting a person's personality and actions in relating to others (Numbers 32:23).

Deception follows a pattern in people. Normally others around them (such as family members or friends) feel they are hiding something or they are not totally transparent. When confronted, the first reaction is to deny the sin or that they could be doing anything wrong. Denial then becomes a stronghold, and it requires them to lie to others to cover their sin. People begin to notice loopholes in their explanations.

Luke 12:2 says, **"For there is nothing covered, that shall not be revealed; neither hid, that shall not be known."** There is also a need to remove oneself from any people who would have a sensitivity or an awareness of their weakness and/or sin. Sometimes they may become critical of these people so that those presently around them won't talk to them and discover something is wrong. For the alcoholic, he must hide his bottle in places of secret from those around him. The drug addict must cover for money he takes to support his habit by lying when asked, "How was it spent?"

In the case of incest, the abuser will use statements to create fear in the abused that would keep them from telling someone and getting help. The abuser usually becomes less of a happy person. They lose the emotion of joy. They normally become used to a life of just existing until their next abusive act. The physical abuser uses statements to create fear in the abused so that the abuse can continue and the abuser can remain in control. In the case of any type of controlling person, statements are used to create fear in the one being controlled so that the controlling person can continue to be manipulative. Pride, of course, is at the root of all of this. These types of people refuse to humble themselves, admit their sin, repent to God and to those they have hurt, and seek help.

True repentance, which I defined for you in chapter 3, according to 2 Corinthians 7:9-11, will cause a person to submit to warning, correction and conviction of sin. True repentance will cause a person to admit, confess and humbly ask forgiveness and cleansing for sin. There is a godly sorrow or remorse that happens in a person over sin when he or she realizes their soul is in danger of hell if the sin is not repented of. Repentance also means to turn from the sin and press after God more than ever. It brings a carefulness or thoughtfulness to obey God. There is a desire to clear oneself from the sin. This may need to involve clearing it with others by going to them or writing to them with a sincere request for forgiveness.

Then it will require walking out carefully, heeding your actions over a period of time to exemplify fruits of repentance.

True repentance also brings an indignation or hatred of the sin repented of. Then it brings a vehement desire to walk right with God and with others, being considerate and lovingly respectful of them. There is then a revenge against the devil now that you know his tactics and your weakness, to stay sober and not let it happen again.

Finally, there is a desire to approve yourself clear in the matter to those over you spiritually and to those all around you. A person involved in incomplete repentance, in frustration will say, "Look, I'm sorry. What more can I say or do?" The person is simply sorry for getting caught but hasn't followed through with the fruits of repentance, willing to prove they have changed. There is no need for frustration, just humility and willingness to do what needs to be done to correct and rebuild.

For example, a spouse commits adultery against his or her mate. He or she admits the sin to the mate and asks forgiveness. The mate forgives and says, "Let's stay together, leave the past and go forward." The mate who hurt the other mate through sinning against him or her must now rebuild trust. There will be several things the mate must do to assure his or her love to be faithful. It could mean calling during the day to say, "You're my one and only and I love you." It could mean coming home for lunch or meeting for lunch, and as soon as the workday is finished, having no after-hour work. It could be to write love notes, send flowers or take the mate on business trips. It will also mean receiving marital counsel for a season. These are practical things, along with transparent communication and seeking God together, that can heal and make a relationship whole again.

> *Fruits of repentance mean you love others so much, like Jesus loves, that you will lay down your life for them to live.*

Although some may be shocked to realize that incest has happened in some who have been church attenders for years, we must wake up to the fact that many hidden sins have gone on in people's lives in churches as well as out of churches. In these last days, however, we are seeing darkness coming to light.

In the case of sexual abuse against a child, true repentance and true agape love will cause a person to do what is best for the abused person. This could mean separating oneself from the other and letting God love the person through you at a distance. Cohabitation could present a possibility of going back into an opportunity for hidden sin again. Fruits of repentance mean you love others so much, like Jesus loves, that you will lay down your life for them to live. Those who want to walk free of deception are willing to be truthful, accountable, and responsible to God and to others. They are willing to sacrifice their own desires for the benefit of saving another.

In a recent city newspaper article on child molestation, a man who had been convicted and served time in prison and had been released was quoted, saying that he realized he could never allow himself to be in a setting where he would be vulnerable again. He also said that after receiving weekly counsel throughout a year and a half time span, he had submitted himself to stay in contact with a counselor in order to keep himself accountable to someone.

The article did not say that this man was a Christian. If someone without Christ has enough moral conscience to act in such a way, how much more should someone who calls himself or herself a Christian act with moral conscience and selfless love toward someone they have victimized.

Whatever a former victimizer does should be after much prayer and counsel, and they should remain in an accountable position for the rest of their life.

God never leads people to do something that victimizes another.

·············(6)·············▶

KEEPING JESUS YOUR CENTER OF FOCUS

*S*elf-deception can come in the form of distractions. If the enemy cannot entice a person into immorality, sometimes he tries to deceive people by distracting them from keeping Jesus as their central focus in life, diverting their mind, abilities and time to something else. This can range all the way from filling one's life with material things, or people, or activities. Even family can sometimes be exalted above a person's love for God.

Jesus said in Luke 21:34-36 AMP to those asking about the signs of the end time:

But take heed to yourselves and be on your guard, lest your hearts be overburdened and depressed (weighed down) with the giddiness and headache and nausea of self-indulgence, drunkenness, and worldly worries and cares pertaining to [the business of] this life, and [lest] that day come upon you suddenly like a trap or a noose;

For it will come upon all who live upon the face of the entire earth.

Keep awake then and watch at all times [be discreet, attentive, and ready], praying that you may have the full strength and ability and

be accounted worthy to escape all these things [taken together] that will take place, and to stand in the presence of the Son of Man. Deuteronomy 11:16 says, **"Take heed to yourselves, that your heart be not deceived, and ye turn aside, and serve other gods, and worship them."** Webster says that an *idol* is "any object of ardent or excessive devotion or admiration."[1] Anything that takes a majority of a person's attention and focus becomes like a god to them.

Many serve (or idolize) the god of sports in our society and because it is healthy, wholesome (most of the time) and families support one another in it, it is considered a very good thing to commit one's life to. The problem emerges when sports take all of your time, ability and attention to the point that church and your relationship with Jesus are put on the back burner. Nothing is wrong with sports unless it robs the first place of Jesus in your life.

We are also living in a time where many are idolizing the physical body. Some spend more time, money and thought toward their physical body than they do toward their spirit. If we stop and think about it, we should realize the early disciples did not focus their minds on their eating and exercise. They were not gluttons, but their lives were given to spread the Gospel. There is nothing wrong with getting some exercise and eating a well-balanced diet. However, if you become consumed with this, you will be spreading the gospel of exercise and diet instead of Jesus. Paul said, **"For bodily exercise prof-**

---

[1] *Webster's New World Dictionary*, New York, NY: Simon & Schuster, 1982, p. 607.

iteth little: but *godliness is profitable unto all things,* **having promise of the life that now is, and of that which is to come."** (See 1 Timothy 4:1-9.) Remember where the emphasis of scripture is.

The Scripture says, **"Thou shalt have no other gods before me"** (Exodus 20:3). When sports, music, food, exercise, academic education, a job, or even family require a Christian to put them first, that Christian is beginning on a road to a backslidden condition. Ultimately, there'll be sports games, school classes, or seminars to enhance one's job, etc. that end up on Sunday and Wednesday. Then there'll be early morning practices or weekend commitments that compromise your time with God or the church. This kind of deception leads to compromise, and compromise leads to losing spirituality. The point I am making is, who or what is first in your life, and who or what determines what you are going to do with your life?

Another form of deception that some Christians do not recognize is the gaining of so much head knowledge or even experiential knowledge that they think they should be recognized in a leadership position over others. A lot of people want to be recognized as the "top dog," but many are not willing

> *A lot of people want to be recognized as the "top dog," but many are not willing to pay the price of serving to get there.*

to pay the price of serving to get there. Remember, Jesus said to His disciples who wanted to know who would be next to Him on a throne in His Kingdom, "Whoever wants to be greatest of all and most important in rank must be a servant to all" (see Matthew 23:11; Luke 9:46-48).

First Corinthians 3:18-21 says:

Let no man deceive himself. If any man among you seemeth to be wise in this world, let him become a fool, that he may be wise.

For the wisdom of this world is foolishness with God. For it is written, He taketh the wise in their own craftiness.

And again, The Lord knoweth the thoughts of the wise, that they are vain.

Therefore let no man glory in men....

Through the years I've had some people come to me with their ministry business cards, reading something like, "Apostle—Prophet—Evangelist—Pastor—Teacher—Rev. John Doe," or "The Most Reverend Bishop Dr. and Head of the World International Church of Jesus Christ," etc. When they have a few weak folks following them who don't know any better, this gives them a sense of having a name and a position.

Jesus said, **"And whosoever of you will be the chiefest, shall be servant of all"** (Mark 10:44). Galatians 6:3 says, **"For if a man think himself to be something, when he is nothing, he deceiveth himself."** If you are an important leader, believe me, you won't have to advertise it. Great people in the church have servant hearts and are led by compassion, not selfish ambition. People are drawn to someone who they feel genuinely loves them and reaches out to help them.

Jesus said, "And whosoever of you will be the chiefest, shall be servant of all" (Mark 10:44).

Once when we were talking with Dr. Cho, pastor of the largest church in the world located in Seoul, Korea, he said, "In America too many want to be chiefs and not enough Indians." He noticed many wanting to be the head pastor or a star evangelist or teacher when some were really called to assist and support others. America has many, who in order not to have to submit, go out and do their own thing. Many of those have had small fruit and had to close down after a period of time. Pride kept them from hooking up with others (who had proven their calling to lead) and thus kept them from having a greater impact in ministry.

Having a servant attitude will help you be in the right ministry calling, blessing many people, and it will keep you from deception.

Deception Through Others

Apart from self-deception, deception can come to a person from the outside through people who are deceptive. Those who are deceptive look for the spiritually young or spiritually weakened (offended) Christians to prey upon. In Matthew 24:4 when the disciples asked Jesus what would be the signs of the end of time, He said to them, **"Take heed that no man deceive you."** There are those who say they are ministers of Christ but are not and through smooth words draw non-discerning Christians to themselves.

Second Corinthians 11:3-4,13-15 TLB says:

But I am frightened, fearing that in some way you will be led away from your pure and simple devotion to our Lord, just as Eve was deceived by Satan in the Garden of Eden. You

seem so gullible: you believe whatever anyone tells you even if he is preaching about another Jesus than the one we preach, or a different spirit than the Holy Spirit you received, or shows you a different way to be saved. You swallow it all...

God never sent those men at all; they are "phonies" who have fooled you into thinking they are Christ's apostles. Yet I am not surprised! Satan can change himself into an angel of light, so it is no wonder his servants can do it too, and seem like godly ministers. In the end they will get every bit of punishment their wicked deeds deserve.

There are some Christians who haven't gained a knowledge of God's Word and experience to discern truth from that which is false or in error. Others are at times weakened by holding an offense toward another Christian or a group of Christians. They then become open target for deceivers to convince them everyone else is just taking advantage of them. They make them feel that they have all the answers and many times invite them to help start a Bible study group that is totally all Christ's Church should be. This kind of exclusive approach should be a "red flag," but some jump on it "hook, line and sinker."

Four primary keys to help you recognize error in cults and deceptive doctrines are:

1. What do they do with Jesus?

    a. Is Jesus the center of their doctrine, is another person the center of it, or does their doctrine center around their own revelation?

b. Do they believe Jesus died and was raised from the dead?

c. Do they recognize Jesus as the only Son of God and the only way to salvation and to heaven?

2. Do they want to add some other book of revelation to the Bible that they believe is necessary and equal with the Bible?

3. Do they want to isolate you from other Christians or churches?

4. Is there a controlling element for being involved in their group?

Matthew 7:20 says we can detect false teachers or ministers by their fruit. Jude and 2 Peter, chapter 2, describe the following characteristics of a false or deceptive teacher: They'll have a spiritual pride of superiority in order not to be challenged. They'll be rebellious and critical toward other spiritual authorities and at times toward governmental authorities. They'll be subject to lust for immorality and sensuality. They'll be covetous of others' possessions, ministries, or spouses. They'll be self-centered. They will lie to cover up truth about themselves. They will have a mixture of truth and error.

Questions that you may ask yourself in order to discern would be: Are there many unsaved receiving Jesus as Lord and Savior through their ministry? Are people being healed in their bodies and lives, delivered from demonic oppression and helped? Does the person teach in such a way that divides people from other Christian churches? Do they want to help people, or do they simply want a following to serve them? Do they make people feel that if they don't follow them and their group, they could go to hell if they went to another church? Do they teach in such a way that makes people feel they are better than others? Do they control people by continually prophesying to them direction for their lives? (See 1 John 4:1.) Do you experience God's compassion or just spiritual charisma when you're around them?

> *God's prophetic words will always line up with His written Word.*

First Corinthians 14:1 says, **"Follow after charity [agape love], and desire spiritual gifts, but rather that ye may prophesy."** First Thessalonians 5:20-21 says, **"Despise not prophesyings. Prove** [or test] **all things; hold fast that which is good** [or right]." Prophecy is to confirm what God speaks to an individual personally. It is not to manipulate or control them. Each believer has their own connection with God and can hear God *if* they abide in the Word and listen to their heart.

We are to judge or examine every prophecy. First Corinthians 13:9-10,12 says, **"For we know *in part*, and we prophesy *in part*. But when that which is perfect is come, then that which is in part shall be done away...then shall [we] know even as also [we are] known."**

Until Jesus' return, we must realize *"all"* prophecy that comes through humans must be judged and determined if it is God speaking or if it is just the desire of the person for others. Anyone who is humble before God is willing to have their words judged and will not be upset by it. If they have spoken beyond what God is wanting to speak, then they should submit to correction by others in spiritual leadership. God's prophetic words will always line up with His written Word. If someone says to do anything the Bible does not say, then you should hold steady and ask God to confirm His will in you.

Is the fruit of the Holy Spirit exhibited in their lives in the way they treat people (including their spouse and children)? Do you see anger and ill will toward others or a manipulative dictator approach? Do you see patience and self-control? Are they self-centered or people-centered? Are they faithful? Do they do whatever it takes to minister to a need by "going the extra mile" with someone? Are they gentle or harsh with people? Are they humble, and do they let God defend them? How do they treat people off the platform or in normal activities? Are they submitted and accountable to any other ministry? These are questions to ask yourself before following after people.

We are living in such difficult times, and there are so many voices speaking all around us. We must become rightly related to other believers, churches and ministries. Ministry organizations must become rightly related one to another for protection from error and deception. Any minister who refuses to be submitted to others in ministry is setting himself up, as well as those who follow him, to be deceived.

Years ago a lady came to our church and began prophesying in our service. Her prophecy was "off base," so my husband asked her to stop. She took offense and began to leave, saying she was "shaking the dust off her feet" from our church (Luke 9:5). Through the years I've heard this scripture quoted out of context a few times by people who were either bitter, moochers, or caught up in spiritual pride.

As she left, one of our staff kindly asked her if she was a member of our church. She quickly replied, "No,

67

I'm not a member of any particular church. I'm a member of the whole Church of God, and I'm on an assignment going from church to church, to prophesy in order to correct them." By this statement, she automatically revealed that she wasn't sent by God but was going around on her own direction.

The Word of God clearly states that we are to be submitted to elders who know us and watch over our souls (Hebrews 13:17). Throughout the New Testament, apostles, prophets, evangelists, pastors and teachers were connected with each other and submitted one to another in the fear of the Lord (Ephesians chapters 4 and 5). This woman's attitude of pride and unwillingness to be corrected were sure signs of "no fruit of the Holy Spirit."

True spiritual people are willing to submit and be corrected when approached by other spiritual leaders whom God has ordained and placed in the Body of Christ.

(Note: In Acts 11 Peter met with other church leadership to explain what happened at Cornelius' house and how the Gospel was for the Gentiles also. He helped the other ministers see their need to embrace non-Jews in the Christian faith. Again in Acts 15, church leaders from all around met to talk through how to handle differences of opinions and work together for the sake of the Gospel. They were not all separated, each doing their own thing with no connection to the rest of the Body of Christ and other leaders.)

Those of us in ministry need to be related or connected with other ministers who can speak into our lives. This is one way to ensure accountability and responsibility. We are not sufficient in our own selves. As 1 Corinthians 12 says, we need one another in the Body of Christ.

EVEN THE ELECT CAN BE DECEIVED

I grew up in a solid Christian home. My father served as a pastor with my mother faithfully serving by his side. Although I thought I loved God and I joined the church as a child, over the years, I had doubts of my salvation. It was at age sixteen that I made an all-out surrender and commitment to Jesus. That night as I released my life to obey God, He spoke to me in my thoughts, "Read your Bible and have a prayer time daily." He also put the thought in me that He had called me into the ministry. I had no comprehension of how it would happen, but a peace came over me that He would lead me one step at a time. Prior to this, in my heart I was seeking a goal of fame and fortune.

God led me not to tell anyone so that I would not be misunderstood. This also began a spiritual hunger in me that has endured even to this very day. There were times when it was not exciting and seemingly just a habit, but that still small voice would say, "*Continue* in My Word." John 8:31-32 says, **"If ye continue in my word, then are ye my disciples indeed; and ye shall know the truth, and the truth shall make you free."** First Timothy 4:16 says, **"Take heed unto thyself, and unto the doctrine; continue in them: for in doing this thou shalt both save thyself, and them that hear thee."**

We, as Christians, must realize that God not only works in the spectacular times to build our lives, but in the everyday routine times as well. Never quit! As I went after Jesus, I surrounded myself with other people who were going after Jesus. Proverbs 27:17 says, **"Iron sharpeneth iron,"** and a person can sharpen another person mentally and spiritually. (The opposite is also true, so I realized I had to avoid relationships that could pull me down.)

As years passed, I observed the people around me going after Jesus and the Word of God and I wondered how any of those people could ever be deceived. I felt sure that there was no opportunity that the devil could get in. However, over the years I've seen some of the people I considered strong at one time become deceived, people I never dreamed could have been deceived. They became **"dull of hearing"** (Hebrews 5:11). **"Wherefore let him that thinketh he standeth take heed lest he fall"** (1 Corinthians 10:12).

One night in January of 1990, I was suddenly awakened from a sound sleep. It was 2:37 a.m. on our clock. I sat up in bed and inside of my spirit I heard a strong voice say to me, "You've wondered how the elect (or strong Christians) could become deceived and I'm going to tell you. They will become slack in pursuing Me in My Word daily, in a daily prayer time, in walking in right-relatedness with others and in giving out of their lives."

Inside of me I felt such an alarm and responsibility to tell others what I sensed God wanted the Body of Christ to awaken to. My husband had me share it with our congregation, and since then, whenever I've spoken to other groups of believers, I've shared it. Some have agreed and

70

received this truth while others have just let it slide, making no effort to apply it. Those who make no effort to act on God's Word open themselves up to become shipwrecked in their faith.

These are the four basic ways of growth that any Christian knows. God spoke to me, "Many will *know* them, but they won't *do* them." He then began to explain and elaborate to me over the next months and years what He meant.

> *Those who make no effort to act on God's Word open themselves up to become shipwrecked in their faith.*

As you read this, my prayer is that it will deliver you and help you to deliver others from deception in these latter days.

THE WORD OF GOD

*T*he Spirit of God spoke within me that many who believe and can even quote Scripture or read a portion of the Word of God as a habit daily will begin to become inconsistent and neglect the Word.

Paul said in 2 Peter 1:12-13 NKJV:

For this reason I will not be negligent to remind you always of these things, though you know and are established in the present truth.

Yes, I think it is right, as long as I am in this tent, to stir you up by reminding you.

The Word of God must become as necessary to us as daily food and must be pursued as much as pursuing an education, a job, a mate, or any other thing we value.

Jesus said in Matthew 4:4, **"...Man shall not live by bread alone, but by every word that proceedeth out of the mouth of God."** We must determine to live by the Word and daily pursue the Word of God.

When you seek God's Word as your daily wisdom, He will be able to work His will in your life. God's Word will be like a measuring stick to you. Everything in your life will be measured, judged and brought in line with His Word. God's Word has a way of exposing the flesh and demanding the flesh to straighten up. His Word will help you discern between your soul (your emotions, mind and will) and your spirit (the inner man where God speaks to you).

Hebrews 4:12 says:

For the word of God is quick, and powerful, and sharper than any twoedged sword, piercing even to the *dividing* asunder of *soul* and *spirit*, and of the joints and marrow, and is a *discerner* of the *thoughts* and *intents* of the heart.

The Word of God will help you discern if your motives are right or if they are selfish. God's Word will convict you if your thoughts are wrong. God's Word will show you actions that are wrong and teach you how to act or live right with God and with others. His Word will put a demand upon us and require responsibility from us for our lives personally and a responsibility toward others. God's Word raises a person's standard of life. No social work or other religion can do this, even though they've tried. When a person commits himself to live by the Word, he will be different than the world around him.

Jesus told His disciples in John 8:31-32 to *continue* in His Word and they would know the truth, and the truth would make them free. Then He said as they continued in His Word, they would be His true disciples. He realized it wasn't enough for them to have lived with Him and traveled and ministered with Him for three years. They had to *continue* in the Word and in the truths He had taught and shown them. Many Christians start off with a "bang" pursuing Jesus, then slack up along the way feeling they've learned enough to coast awhile. You can't coast. You're either pressing forward or sliding back. There's no parking

> *God's Word raises a person's standard of life.*

spot. Though you may have read through the Bible fifteen times, it always brings life and light to you. The Word of God is not like a novel to be read once or twice. It is living and has power to transform us.

The definition of *continue* is "to go on or extend; stretch; to go on in a course of action or condition; to endure, resisting destructive influences or forces; to persist in; to abide."[1] John 15:1-11 says, "If you abide in Me and My words abide in you, you'll be cleansed through My Word each time you receive it; you'll bear more fruit; you'll ask in prayer according to My will and it will be done; you'll abide in My love; and your joy will be full."

Jeremiah 15:16 says, **"Thy words were found, and I did eat them** [received them and chose to act on them]**; and thy word was unto me the joy and rejoicing of mine heart...."** If we're really disciples of Jesus, we'll continue in His Word. This means not only hearing it preached and reading it, but making a decision to live by it in every aspect of life.

James 1:22-25 says:

But be ye *doers* of the word, and not hearers only, deceiving your own selves.

For if any be a hearer of the word, and not a doer, he is like unto a man beholding his natural face in a glass:

For he beholdeth himself, and goeth his way, and straightway forgetteth what manner of man he was.

But whoso looketh into the perfect law of liberty [the Word]**, and *continueth* therein, he being**

---

[1]   *Webster's New World Dictionary*, New York, NY: Simon & Schuster, 1982, p. 308.

not a forgetful hearer, but a doer of the work, this man shall be blessed in his deed.

You can't expect to be like Jesus or to be blessed of God if you don't continue in His Word. His blessings will lift from you if you stop continuing in His Word.

A person who had left ministry over offenses told me

> *Jesus never said, "Pack in the Word of God and then coast."*

that their spouse was no longer reading the Bible daily. When asked about it, the spouse replied, "I studied my Bible at least two hours or more daily for several years, and I think I put enough in me to coast awhile."

Jesus never said, "Pack in the Word of God and then coast." He did say, however, in John 15 to *abide* in His Word and let His Word *abide* in you. He also said in John 14:23-24, "If a man loves Me, he'll keep My Word, but if he does not keep My Word, he does not really love Me." Jesus and the Word are one and the same. To say we love Jesus but we don't love His Word is to lie. Loving His Word is not just reading it daily but making the effort to obey it.

If a person said, "I love you" to his mate and then said, "but I don't want to listen to you or do what you say," then his mate would realize he doesn't really love them. As we love Jesus, we will love His Word. We keep our eyes on Jesus as we keep our eyes on His Word.

Hebrews 12:2-3 says we are to *keep our eyes on Jesus* and always *consider* Him and what He would do and what His Word says. Jesus taught and lived by principles that show us how to walk in the light as He is in the light and how to avoid deception and snares of the devil.

God's words are able to help us determine (or discern) what is of the soul (our own emotions, mind and will or desires) and what is of the spirit (where the Holy Spirit speaks to the inner man of the heart). His words are so alive and powerful that they can heal (Proverbs 4:20-22). His words can free a person from wrong habits and wrong desires (John 8:32). His words can cleanse our minds and keep us from sinning (Psalm 119:9,11).

The Word of God is not like a history book to be read once for information or even to memorize some facts. The Word of God is *life* to us (Proverbs 4:20-22). It gives us life and is always capable of changing us when we read it with a desire to be changed (Romans 12:2).

Jesus was very aware of our need to abide or continue in His Word in order to walk in the fruit of His Spirit. In John 15:1-11, He said that if we quit abiding in His Word and we quit letting His Word abide in us, then we would not be able to bear His fruit and we would not be able to abide in His love toward others around us. He also said in order for our joy to remain in us through difficult times as well as good times that it was contingent on our abiding in His Word and in His love.

Have you ever noticed how you can be peaceful or joyful for a season in your life and then begin to allow those old attitudes of fear, worry, anger, strife, or pride to creep back in? Usually it is when you get too busy for time in the Word of God.

Our salvation depends upon abiding or continuing in Him. The reason is that if we don't abide or continue in His Word, the enemy will come and take us in a weak point when least expected.

Hebrews 2:1-3 AMP says:

Since all this is true, we ought to pay much closer attention than ever to the truths that we have heard, lest in any way we drift past [them] and slip away.

For if the message given through angels [the Law spoken by them to Moses] was authentic and proved sure, and every violation and disobedience received an appropriate (just and adequate) penalty,

How shall we escape [appropriate retribution] if we neglect and refuse to pay attention to such a great salvation [as is now offered to us, letting it drift past us forever]? For it was declared at first by the Lord [Himself], and it was confirmed to us and proved to be real and genuine by those who personally heard [Him speak].

In 1974 I heard a teaching from the Navigators that has helped me through the years in putting God's Word in me. Consider that you are holding a Bible. There are five ways that will enable you to hold on to the Word of God where it cannot be taken from you, as illustrated in the following diagram.

If I only hear the Word, it is like trying to hold the Bible with only my thumb. If I hear and read the Word, the Bible could be easily knocked out of my hand. Notice, the more fingers of my hand that are involved in holding the Bible, the less likely that the Word of God could be taken from me or knocked out of my life because of sin, offense, distraction, or some other deception.

The enemy (Satan) knows if he can pull you away

Read the Word
Revelation 1:3

Study the Word
2 Timothy 2:15

Memorize the Word
Psalm 119:11

Meditate &
Confess the Word
Joshua 1:8
Psalm 1:3

Hear the Word
Romans 10:17

from the Word of God, then he has you in a weakened position to move in. In Mark 4:3-20, Jesus gives the parable of the sower sowing the seed. He said if you can understand this parable, you'll be able to understand all other parables. The seed is the Word of God. When the Word is heard, it can fall on the soil of people's hearts in different ways. If a person only comes to a church service and hears the Word of God preached and thinks it is good, but they don't make a decision to act on it, they are like seed sown by the wayside. Satan comes immediately and takes away the Word that was sown in their hearts. They remain unchanged.

Consider another person who hears the Word of God and immediately makes a decision to believe it and act on it with gladness. However, they begin to experience difficulties, offenses and hard times. They may even receive some persecution for the fact that they have told everyone how Jesus has changed them and worked miracles for them, but now things are seemingly falling

apart. We must realize, these
tests of offenses, hard times
and persecutions come *"for
the Word's sake."* The enemy
brings these to test whether
you are rooted in the Word or
if you are just riding on the
"highs" of other Christians

> *Your attitude
> toward the Word
> will determine
> your ability to
> resist offenses.*

that you are hanging out with. It's not enough to just
attend lots of meetings, we must individually put God's
Word in us daily.

Psalm 119:165 says, **"Great peace have they which
love thy law** [God's Word]: **and nothing shall offend
them."** Your attitude toward the Word will determine
your ability to resist offenses.

The third example given is the person who hears the
Word of God and may even start out having a daily time
reading and praying, but after awhile the enemy sends
distractions or lusts for other things to choke the Word
they've received. Many good Christians choose to not let
offenses or hard times pull them away from the Word or
the church, but they become busy doing good things that
cause them to neglect quiet time with God.

Luke 10:38-42 says:

> **Now it came to pass, as they went, that he
> entered into a certain village: and a certain woman
> named Martha received him into her house.**
>
> **And she had a sister called Mary, which also
> sat at Jesus' feet, and heard his word.**
>
> **But Martha was cumbered about much serv-
> ing, and came to him, and said, Lord, dost thou
> not care that my sister hath left me to serve**

alone? bid her therefore that she help me.

And Jesus answered and said unto her, Martha, Martha, thou art careful and troubled about many things:

But one thing is needful: and Mary hath chosen that good part, which shall not be taken away from her.

We must take some time to sit at Jesus' feet for prayer and for time in the Word. Otherwise, we'll make wrong decisions that will cost us.

Another device is lusts. The enemy sends people into a Christian's path (sometimes even other Christians) who draw on a person emotionally to the point of making them choose between their love of God and them. Then, sometimes it is lusts for getting more things, or making more money with the thought of it ultimately being for the Kingdom of God, but losing sight of sowing into the works of God along the way. Many have been "shipwrecked" because of this deception of Satan. God wants to prosper you, but He doesn't want you to ever desire prosperity more than *Him*. He wants to be *your desire*, then He will bless you.

Matthew 6:33 says:

But seek ye first the kingdom of God, and his righteousness; and all these things shall be added unto you.

The last example of soil is the person who hears and receives the Word of God. This person makes a decision to seek God's Word individually for their personal life, and stay with it through the good and bad times, offenses, persecutions and temptations. This person allows the Word to rule them in their emotions, purposes, direction, goals, relationships and desires. Therefore, they yield fruit in their life that remains.

Each week millions of people attend churches all around the world. Church attendance is not only a good habit that benefits a person positively, but it is a necessity for "the Christian" in these last days as we see the day of the Lord approaching (Hebrews 10:25). However, attending a church service in itself cannot keep you nor will you be able to rightly discern what is preached or taught from a pulpit unless you have a desire to study the Word of God personally. You do not have to go to seminary or even to a Bible school to be a student of the Word of God.

Jesus calls each believer to become *a disciple*, not just a follower (John 8:31-32). He had many followers at times, but they left Him when He wasn't going the direction they wanted to go, or when He began teaching them that He was the living bread from heaven and through His blood they could have eternal life (John 6:66). Some followed Him as long as He taught and demonstrated miracles, healing and deliverance. However, they could not see themselves committing their lives to Him which could cost them being kicked out of the synagogue and later branded as "Christians." Those who identified with Jesus Christ laid down their lives.

A *disciple* is "a person who is a learner." *Disciple* comes from the Greek word, *matheteuo,* which means "to learn, from the root word *math,* indicating thought accompanied by endeavor."[2] It is one who endeavors to learn. A disciple is not only a learner but also an adherent (devoted to follow without deviating or turning

---

[2] *Vine, W. E. An Expository Dictionary of New Testament Words,* Nashville, TN: Thomas Nelson, Publishers, p. 308.

away). Hence, they were spoken of as imitators of their
teacher (John 8:31; 15:8). Webster's Dictionary gives
another definition of *disciple* as "a person who believes
in and helps disseminate (or spread) the teachings of a
master."[3]

When we come to church to hear the Word of God
preached, we should come with the attitude of learning,
releasing faith in the Word, being willing to obey and
adjust our lives to the Word of God and spreading the
Word to others. Paul noted the Bereans' church over the
Thessalonians' church because they received the Word of
God with all readiness of mind and searched the scriptures daily to see if the things Paul preached were so
(Acts 17:10-11).

Even though I've heard my husband preach at least
three times or more each week for over twenty years, I
still take notes on what he speaks and examine the scriptures. I'm his most ardent supporter, but I realize my
need to search the scriptures. At times he will say to people, "Don't just accept what I say without looking at the
scriptures yourself." Both he and I have realized that in
years past, some people have accepted everything that
comes from a pulpit as the Gospel when there were
man's opinions infiltrated into the messages that were
preached. Because of some Christians' lack of study,
they've accepted wrong perspectives of the Word of God
that have bound their lives instead of freeing them or
they've gone into error that has devastated them.

Many years ago, a couple we had known before we
received the baptism of the Holy Spirit, came to us to tell

[3] *Webster's II New Riverside Dictionary*, Boston, MA: Houghton Mifflin
Co., 1984, p. 201.

us that the gifts and manifestations of the Holy Spirit in
1 Corinthians chapters 12-14 were no longer for today but
had ceased. They opened their Bibles and turned to Acts
2:1-4; Acts 10:46; Acts 19:6; 1 Corinthians 14:2,5,13,26-
28; and Isaiah 28:11, where they had put an "x" marking
over those scriptures and had written in the side column,
"Not for today." They had heard their pastor make this
statement, who had his seminary doctorate degree in the-
ology. We were shocked that they had marked out these
scriptures, for Revelation 22:19 says:

**And if any man shall take away from the
words of the book of this prophecy, God shall
take away his part out of the book of life, and
out of the holy city, and from the things which
are written in this book.**

Needless to say, they did not convince us, but rather
gave us a greater desire to search the scriptures which
affirm that the gifts and manifestations of the Holy Spirit
are for today and to study the book of Acts again. In fact,
every writer of the New Testament experienced this baptism of the Holy Spirit with the evidence of speaking in
other tongues. If they all needed this help from the Holy
Spirit, how much more do we need the Holy Spirit's
supernatural help in our lives today!

Another aspect of hearing the Word of God is when
people go door to door witnessing. It is great when
Christians go door to door simply helping people get
saved and inviting them to go to church. However, there
are other groups outside of Christianity who go door to
door. Christians who have not studied the Word of God
at times have become confused or convinced to join their
group. Normally, the Mormons and Jehovah Witnesses

go door to door. They have very sweet people witnessing who apparently are not aware of the deceptions of their group.

Jesus Christ is the only way to heaven (John 14:6). It is *not by our works* that we are saved but *by our faith in the cleansing blood of Jesus*

> *It is not by our own might, power, or abilities, but by His Spirit that we can do the works of Jesus (Zechariah 4:6).*

(Ephesians 2:8). If we are saved by our good works, then Jesus died and shed His blood in vain. Our good works could never measure up to the price Jesus paid to save you and me. Our good works are what we do after we've accepted the saving grace of Jesus (Philippians 2:12-13). It now becomes God in us working out of our lives His will and His good pleasure. It is not by our own might, power, or abilities, but by His Spirit that we can do the works of Jesus (Zechariah 4:6). His Holy Spirit comes into our lives when we are born again (John 3:5-6, 1 Corinthians 12:3). Instead of trying to keep the law in our own ability, at the new birth He puts His law in our hearts and minds (Hebrews 8:10). Then His Holy Spirit speaks inside of our hearts, showing us right and wrong. Most of these people from the two groups I've mentioned have observed Christians living wrong lifestyles so they don't understand if the Holy Spirit is in a Christian to lead them to do good, then why do they do wrong? This is because of Christians neglecting to put the Word in their lives daily. An unrenewed mind is open target to the enemy to bring temptation to sin. With no resisting ability in the person being tempted, they will act out the sin. We must renew our minds to God's Word (Romans 12:1-2; Ephesians 4:23).

When someone says to you that they have another book of revelation that was added along with the Bible and that it is a continuation of the Bible, that should be an immediate "red flag" warning you against it.

Revelation 22:18 says:

For I testify unto every man that heareth the words of the prophecy of this book, If any man shall add unto these things, God shall add unto him the plagues that are written in this book.

Many people have been deceived into thinking this is a good thing and miss the truth of the Gospel of Jesus Christ, thus missing heaven. First John 4:1 says, **"Beloved, believe not every spirit, but try the spirits whether they are of God: because many false prophets are gone out into the world."**

I realize that the enemy tries to distract or deceive, but we can choose to abide or continue in the Word and remain fixed in our hearts. Jesus said, **"But he that shall endure unto the end, the same shall be saved"** (Matthew 24:13).

PRAYER
(THE PRAYER RELATIONSHIP)

*P*rayer is the Christian's lifeline. It is a two-way communication between us and God. It requires talking to God and listening to Him. It is not only a time set apart in our day nor is it just at meals. Prayer is having an open communication line all day and through the night where you or God can speak whenever necessary.

First Peter 4:7 says, **"But the end of all things is at hand: be ye therefore sober, and watch unto prayer."** Jesus said in Luke 18:1 NIV, **"...that they should always pray and not give up."** In other words, don't quit praying. If the enemy can distract you from praying by keeping you too busy, he will. Another tactic of his is to make you feel like nothing is happening.

The Bible says Daniel was in a habit of praying three times daily (Daniel 6:10). For years he and his people were held in another kingdom, and yet he kept his prayer relationship with God. We, of course, know only a few major prayer events in his life, but consider all the years he lived, along with other Jews, under the rule of others who weren't in covenant with God and yet he was mighty in his influence. His prayer life carried him when there were days and months that it looked like nothing was happening. Don't stop praying when you can't see anything happening.

The Scripture indicates that Daniel's prayer life obviously affected his entire personality. The king considered him to be *wiser* and *positioned him above all the other government overseers under him.* He was *faithful.* He had an *excellent spirit* and people *could not find anything bad in his life for which they could accuse him.*

Daniel had a test in his prayer life several times.

> *Because of no compromise, he [Daniel] was put into a lions' den which appeared to be the end. However, it was just an opportunity for his "Prayer Partner" [God] to come on the scene and deliver him with honor.*

Because he was in a prayer relationship with God, he was able to interpret the king's dream, saving his life and the lives of others. Loyalty to his prayer life was tested and he didn't compromise. Because of no compromise, he was put into a lions' den which appeared to be the end. However, it was just an opportunity for his "Prayer Partner" (God) to come on the scene and deliver him with honor.

Another time because of his prayer life, he was able to interpret God's handwriting on a wall to a king. The last record of the effects of his staying with prayer all through his life was that he heard from God concerning the last days of earth. While setting aside time to fast and pray, God spoke to him.

(Note: The combination of fasting and prayer brings a streamlined focus of our heart, mind and body toward God. During this time, a person becomes even more sensitive to God. The body is required to omit the distraction of eating and digesting the food. The whole human system is free of being slowed down. Fasting is not a fad to play with. You should not fast twenty-one days or forty days because Daniel, Moses, or Jesus did it. You should fast *according to the leading of the Holy Spirit.* Never tempt God. Remember, in Matthew 4:1 Jesus was *led by the Holy Spirit* when He went into the wilderness, fasting and praying through His testing time from the enemy.)

A friend once told me how the Lord had led her on a fifteen-day fast (with only water and juice) for a particular situation. After fifteen days, she felt so good she thought that she'd go ahead and fast twenty-one days like Daniel. By the sixteenth day she began to feel strange. On the seventeenth day, she realized she was being affected mentally and emotionally and was losing control. She immediately broke the fast, but even then found it hard to eat because she had lost her appetite. She said to me, "If I had gone any longer, I would have had to check myself into the psychiatric ward of a hospital." She repented for tempting God, and I prayed for her strength and for God's healing power to restore her to wholeness. Fasting and prayer are tremendous tools for spiritual breakthroughs. Some have never even attempted to pray and fast. Let God direct you.

Never be condemned in your fasting, but let it be a time of drawing close to Jesus and not just doing without certain foods or mealtimes. God leads people differently in their fasting. Some have disdained others for not fasting in the way they fast. The important thing is fasting according to the leading of the Holy Spirit and praying during this time. The two coupled together bring greater sensitivity to the Spirit and to others around you. (If you desire to understand fasting and prayer in a greater depth, we can recommend some books on this topic.)

On his last recorded prayer incident, Daniel prayed uninterrupted for twenty-one days. On the last day of that time period, an angel appeared to him and said he was sent the first day Daniel began praying. He then said he fought with the prince of Persia twenty-one days. However, another great angel, Michael, came and helped him overcome the demonic prince. It was Daniel's persistent prayer that helped bring him on through with the answer.

I believe Jesus is telling all of us in Luke 18:1, don't quit, but keep having a prayer life. Have a time set apart to pray and read the Word of God each day. Then, through the day keep sober to pray instantly and respond to difficult situations with prayer. Remember, prayer is letting God talk, too. (Not just you doing all the talking!)

Years ago a man came to me praying in tongues, and he said, "Have you ever met (then tongues) anyone (then tongues) who prays without ceasing (then he continued in tongues as he looked at me)?" I looked at him in wonder and amazement. Sometimes people misunderstand Scripture. I said, "Yes, but a person who prays without ceasing according to 1 Thessalonians 5:17 does not do *all* the talking." I then explained to him how prayer should be spent at least three-fourths of the time in our listening because God has much greater wisdom to say to us than we have to Him. Remember, He speaks in His written Word and to our thoughts, and all of what He speaks will line up with His written Word (His known will).

First Peter 4:7 says, **"But the end of all things is at hand: be ye therefore sober, and watch unto prayer."**

The signs of the end of times are all around us. Wake up! Listen to your spirit. God will speak into your heart with small thoughts or warnings. Learn to listen and obey them. This is soberness. You won't be taken advantage of if you're alert. Spiritual dullness will cause you to make wrong decisions.

Pray in agreement with God. Don't pray your own reasoning. *Pray God's Word, which is His written will.*

First John 5:14-15 says:

And this is the confidence that we have in him, that, if we ask any thing according to his will, he heareth us:

And if we know that he hear us, whatsoever we ask, we know that we have the petitions that we desired of him.

Allow the Holy Spirit to search your heart in prayer. He will show you anything you need to repent of or change. If our heart doesn't condemn us, we have confidence toward God in prayer (1 John 3:21). His ears are open to the righteous and His eyes are over them (1 Peter 3:12).

Prayerlessness creates an open opportunity for temptation or weakness. **"Watch and pray, that ye enter not into temptation: the spirit indeed is willing, but the flesh is weak"** (Matthew 26:41). Jesus realized this. He had a time of prayer early in the morning and then late in the evening, but He was in tune in prayer throughout the day while He did other things.

Ephesians 6:18 says, **"Praying always with all prayer...."** Prayer involves many components. Philippians 4:6-7 speaks of *supplication*. This is making requests of God for your material, physical and spiritual needs and everything that concerns you in life. The Scripture goes on to say that we should ask with *thanksgiving.* Thanksgiving is where you release your faith that He heard you and that He will meet your needs. Thanksgiving *believes and receives* when prayer is made, not after the answer comes. Thanksgiving simply thanks God ahead of time.

> **Therefore I say unto you, What things soever ye desire, when ye pray, believe that ye receive them, and ye shall have them.**
>
> **Mark 11:24**

Praise and thanksgiving are forms of prayer. Worship is also a form of intimate prayer. Worship adores, honors and loves God the Father. In worship, God can speak thoughts into our hearts of comfort, love, encouragement, rebuke and correction, strength and direction. Some have never learned that praise and worship are forms of prayer. Remember, Psalm 22:3 says God inhabits the praises of His people. The enemy is stilled or stopped in praise and worship (Psalm 8:2; Matthew 21:16). This is why he tries to keep people from praise and especially from worship. The anointing of God flows and destroys Satan's yokes in praise and worship.

Prayer involves intercession (1 Timothy 2:1). Intercession is praying for or standing in the gap for others. Paul exhorts us in 1 Timothy to pray for those

> *In worship, God can speak thoughts into our hearts of comfort, love, encouragement, rebuke and correction, strength and direction.*

in leadership with petitions, prayers and intercessions, and then move into thanksgiving. Notice again, the Word says thanksgiving is to follow your intercession. God's power can be released for others in thanksgiving.

Another part of prayer is praying in tongues. Paul said, **"...I will pray with the spirit, and I will pray with the understanding also..."** (1 Corinthians 14:15). In fact, Paul says in 1 Corinthians 14:39, **"...forbid not to speak with tongues."** Tongues help us at times when we don't know how to pray in our known language but we sense the need to pray for a situation or just to pray. Sometimes we don't know what we need to pray, so the Holy Spirit helps us as we yield to Him and pray in tongues.

Romans 8:26-27 says:

Likewise the Spirit also helpeth our infirmities: for we know not what we should pray for as we ought: but the Spirit itself maketh intercession for us with groanings which cannot be uttered.

And he that searcheth the hearts knoweth what is the mind of the Spirit, because he maketh intercession for the saints according to the will of God.

I'm thankful for tongues because the Holy Spirit has helped me pray many times when I didn't know what to pray. Sometimes He will speak thoughts to you after praying in tongues that let you know who or what you were praying for. Sometimes He uses us to pray in tongues and we don't know all that we have prayed but we have a sense of lifting afterward and a peace that whatever it is, it is in His hands and He's taking care of it. (If you are interested in understanding more on the subject of tongues, please write to us.)

Another part of prayer is the prayer of agreement. Matthew 18:19-20 says:

Again I say unto you, That if two of you shall agree on earth as touching any thing that they shall ask, it shall be done for them of my Father which is in heaven.

For where two or three are gathered together in my name, there am I in the midst of them.

There's power in two people agreeing together in prayer for answers and for miracles to happen.

Matthew 18:18 also mentions binding and loosing. Of course, we realize in this context He is speaking on forgiveness and unforgiveness. However, in prayer we can bind the devil in Jesus' name and loose people or situations for God to work in them.

And I will give unto thee the keys of the kingdom of heaven: and whatsoever thou shalt bind on earth shall be bound in heaven: and whatsoever thou shalt loose on earth shall be loosed in heaven.

Matthew 16:19

Mark 16:17-18 tells us of the authority we've been given as believers in Jesus' name to cast the devils out and free people. In prayer we can bind or stop the enemy's influence momentarily and loose people for God to work in them.

Prayer involves so many facets, but it is basically letting God be involved all the time in your life and through your life.

Prayer is a combination of a set aside time and "in tuneness" throughout the day and night. Sometimes the

Spirit of God will speak to you in your sleep to awake and pray. Sometimes you may not know why you have an urgency to pray in the Spirit, but obey and pray. You could be the prayer connection to God for someone in need.

There has been great teaching on prayer and the different kinds of prayer. The important thing is to pray. God doesn't expect you to pray like someone else. He just wants you to pray from your own sincere heart and learn from others who've been consistent in prayer. Stop comparing yourself with others who pray. God will work with every level of Christian praying. He's so merciful, He'll teach us as well as answer us as we pray. His answers may not be exactly how we planned it, but if we don't stop praying and believing His Word, He'll cause things to come into divine order.

Prayer involves many components: praise and worship; supplication; thanksgiving; intercession for others; binding and loosing; speaking the Word to mountains of difficulty; agreeing with others for specific needs; trust and rest in faith; praying in the Spirit (tongues) and in the understanding (your known language); listening to your spirit and to the written Word of God; and meditation and agreeing with the Word as you pray.

If you're going to make it in life, you need to talk with your Creator and Savior. He'll be your guide, strengthener, encourager, comforter, healer, friend, restorer, helper, counselor, provider and protector. He will also be your source of cleansing, freedom and victory.

RIGHT-RELATEDNESS

*T*he third area in which the Lord told me people would become deceived is in the area of right-relatedness. There is so much involved in right-relatedness that you will notice this chapter is longer than any other chapter. The other three areas are just as vital, but more has been taught and written on them than on this area. For this reason, I have expounded on this particular area of being rightly related to God and to others as a Christian.

The Lord impressed upon my heart that some people would either stop going to church or would regularly change churches, never getting rooted into a church. He spoke within my heart that Christians had to have *"right-relatedness."* He was not just talking to me about "fellowship," but *"right-relatedness."* Fellowship never requires people to become rightly related. It is simply a gathering of people in a friendly setting around a common interest. Fellowship can happen with a crowd of people who never really get to know one another. God emphasized to me that there are many Christians who attend church but will fall away because of never becoming rightly related in the Body of Christ.

For example, when people simply fellowship and never become rightly related with others, if they go through a difficult experience, they don't feel comfortable telling someone else they've not established a relationship with. They end up suffering alone instead of receiving the strength and help of others.

We need to also be aware that just as it was in the New Testament (Acts 20:28-31, Jude 3-25), today there are some who come into churches (not just large churches but smaller churches also), who deceptively want to appear that they are a part of the group in order to draw away immature or weak Christians to take advantage of them. If a believer is not rightly related with others in the church, they may not be able to discern these people and end up following them.

There are many reasons we need to be rightly related in a local church. Some have thought they could simply watch TV as their church. The problem with this is that when they are sick, down and out, having family problems or there is a death in the family, who do they call on TV to come see them or help them? Many do not live close enough to those that they watch on TV to get someone to come. They also miss the joy of knowing others in the Lord and having those friendships. We need all the TV ministry that is touching and reaching people. But we also need to be related within a local church where we can be physically present to help one another.

Hindrances to Right-Relatedness

Allow me to share with you some hindrances to right-relatedness.

One word that has been difficult for people, especially in America, to accept and walk in, is *submission*. In order to be rightly related to God and to others, we will have to become submissive. Webster defines *submission* as "to voluntarily yield to another; to surrender one's own plans or direction to another; to commit to the discretion or decision of another or of others."[1] It is bringing oneself under the leadership of another.

First, Submit to God

Right-relatedness to God means you must yield yourself to God and place yourself under His leadership and authority.

James 4:6-7 says:

...**God resisteth the proud, but giveth grace** [favor and help] **unto the humble.**

Submit yourselves therefore to God. **Resist the devil, and he will flee from you.**

Submission requires humility. God won't humble you. You must humble yourself. Then you will submit to His direction, His thoughts, His corrections and His flow. When you are in submission to God, you can resist the devil's temptations and testings and overcome them like Jesus did in Matthew 4. Submission is a *daily* decision and act. It requires dying to self in order to live in a way that influences others around you toward Jesus. Once you begin learning how to submit properly, then authority will flow in your life against the devil.

> *When you are in submission to God, you can resist the devil's temptations and testings and overcome them like Jesus did in Matthew 4.*

---

[1] *Webster's New World Dictionary*, New York, NY: Simon & Schuster, 1982, p. 746.

In Luke 7:1-10, the centurion recognized that Jesus was a man under authority, and thus He had authority in the Spirit to speak and sickness would obey Him. He told Jesus to just speak the Word and his servant, who was miles away, would be healed.

> *God wants His people on earth to walk in authority over sin, sickness and any other oppression of the devil.*

God wants His people on earth to walk in authority over sin, sickness and any other oppression of the devil. However, we must keep ourselves in check to make sure we are submitting to Him.

Many times small things that we allow to slide by or don't obey His still small voice in, gradually clog the pipeline from heaven to us and our authority diminishes.

Song of Solomon 2:15 says, **"...the little foxes...spoil the vines."** Make a decision to submit to Him in small things as well as in big things.

Second, Submit to God's Word

Many Christians feel they are submitted to God and can quote James 4:7 very religiously. However, over the years I've watched people submit with their mouth but not with their heart and lives.

Jesus said:

> **These people draw near to Me with their mouth, and honor Me with their lips, but their heart is far from Me.**
>
> **And in vain they worship Me, teaching as doctrines the commandments of men.**
>
> **Matthew 15:8-9** NKJV

If we say we're submitting to God, then we will submit to His Word. God and His Word are one. Some only want to submit to a portion of the Word of God. They quickly defend themselves if someone tries to point out where they may need to adjust their lives in another area of Jesus' instructions in living.

For example, I've known people who were church attenders, tithers, had prayer and Bible reading time daily, but had prejudice in their hearts toward people of another color. Their conversation and attitudes revealed their prejudice to others around them. Little jokes about people of another color or descriptive names that they never corrected but continued using allowed others to know just how they felt on the inside.

We could carry this thought over into the realm of vulgar jokes about anyone. Jesus said in Matthew 12:36, **"...every idle word that men shall speak, they shall give account thereof in the day of judgment."** Check your conversation. Is it profitable?

Ephesians 4:29-32 says:

> **Let no corrupt communication proceed out of your mouth, but that which is good to the use of edifying, that it may minister grace unto the hearers.**
>
> **And grieve not the holy Spirit of God, whereby ye are sealed unto the day of redemption.**
>
> **Let all bitterness, and wrath, and anger, and clamour, and evil speaking, be put away from you, with all malice:**
>
> **And be ye kind one to another, tenderhearted, forgiving one another, even as God for Christ's sake hath forgiven you.**

Sometimes Christians attend church, possibly serve as an usher or a Sunday school teacher, have a daily Bible reading and prayer time, and yet have uncontrolled anger at home. I've known of verbal and physical abuse that has gone on in so-called "Christian" homes, confusing children to think that this is normal and that all parents act this way. WRONG! I've known of people in ministry who've allowed themselves to function in this style of parenting. Sometimes a man makes the wife and children feel it's either their fault for his anger or it's his stressful lifestyle. *It's nobody's fault but the one who is uncontrolled and unsubmitted.*

> *Each of us is individually responsible for our own thoughts, attitudes and actions.*

A Christian does not have the privilege of blaming others for their emotional state of being. Each of us is individually responsible for our own thoughts, attitudes and actions. It's time to accept responsibility for our own faults, repent and ask for help. The Scripture bears out that Jesus will come back to receive to Himself *those who have overcome.* We as Christians must rise up and recognize the enemy's devices that attempt to keep us from overcoming to the end.

These are just two scriptures that some people avoid. There are many more. The point I am making is, though we willingly submit to one portion of scripture we like, we're commanded to submit to the entire counsel and commands of God's Word. These commands are not to be grievous (1 John 5:3). Instead, they are to help us live a better life here on earth, overcome to the end and be a witness of the life of Jesus to others who do not know Him. How can we win others to Him if they see things in us that are just like the world they live in?

> *How can we win others to Him if they see things in us that are just like the world they live in?*

Many Christians hear and believe John 10:10, how that Jesus came to give us a more abundant life, but they aren't experiencing it. Some simply blame the devil for everything and resign to the fact that they are just one of those who has more attacks from the devil than others.

Since our society blames everything and everyone else for its problems, this kind of Christian never searches his or her own heart to see if he or she has a fault in some area that is hindering the abundant life God promised. Some mistakenly think abundant life is having a lot of money, new and expensive cars, a nice house, a handsome husband or a beautiful wife who is in marvelous physical shape, working when they want to work and taking leisure days whenever they want if they don't feel like working. WAKE UP! This is not the abundant life Jesus spoke about. This is TV fantasy.

Abundant life is:

1. Having a close fellowship and relationship with God through Jesus Christ.

2. Being able to hear His voice daily and respond to Him, not just living your life by your own little thinking and reasoning.

3. Having your needs met, but even more, so that you can reach out to meet others' needs. Achieving prosperity

takes place over a process of time through faithful sowing and reaping. It is sowing into the Kingdom of God to help the church and the five-fold ministry gifts as they reach people with the Gospel. God wants to prosper you as your soul is prospering (3 John 2).

4. Walking in His redemptive healing provision, whether you are healed and whole or you are in the process of receiving healing. He provided it for us (Isaiah 53:4-5; Matthew 8:16-17; 1 Peter 2:24).

5. Walking in peace toward those around you.

6. Walking in agape love, which is unselfish, giving, forgiving, kind, patient, humble, full of faith for others and willing to go the extra mile with others (1 Corinthians 13:4-8).

7. Having peace of mind instead of confusion, strife, fear, worry, or doubt.

8. Walking in faith with a positive attitude instead of a negative attitude. Believing all things are possible.

9. Having a family who loves God and loves each other.

10. Seeing God's miracle-working power daily all around you in small things as well as in big things. Having a faith attitude instead of a doubt, worry and fear attitude.

11. Walking in His victory that He already accomplished for you through His death and resurrection from the dead. Having *no more shame, guilt, or condemnation* for your past failures, defeat, or sin, but instead walking in righteousness (right standing with God), peace and joy in the Holy Ghost (Romans 14:17).

12. *Moving in His divine flow to others.* Being able to lead someone to Jesus, to pray the prayer of healing over someone and see His power work, to pray deliverance for

someone in bondage and see them free, to hear from God how to help someone else and see them blessed by your obedience.

Some Christians live a miserable life instead of an abundant life because they refuse to operate according to the principles of God's Word. When His Word says, **"Casting all your care upon him..."** (1 Peter 5:7), they keep their care and nurse it. Although His Word says, **"...Love your enemies, bless them that curse you, do good to them that hate you, and pray for them which despitefully use you, and persecute you"** (Matthew 5:44), some Christians *sue* the people who hurt them or make them go through a difficult time. Instead of walking in the love of Jesus, they walk in **"...An eye for an eye, and a tooth for a tooth"** concept (Matthew 5:38). Instead of treating others with the mercy they want to be treated with, they hurt them.

First Corinthians 6:1-8 says:

> **Dare any of you, having a matter against another, go to law before the unjust, and not before the saints?**
>
> **Do ye not know that the saints shall judge the world? and if the world shall be judged by you, are ye unworthy to judge the smallest matters?**
>
> **Know ye not that we shall judge angels? how much more things that pertain to this life?**
>
> **If then ye have judgments of things pertaining to this life, set them to judge who are least esteemed in the church.**
>
> **I speak to your shame. Is it so, that there is not a wise man among you? no, not one that**

**shall be able to judge between his brethren?
But brother goeth to law with brother, and
that before the unbelievers.
Now therefore there is utterly a fault among
you, because ye go to law one with another.
Why do ye not rather take wrong? why do ye
not rather suffer yourselves to be defrauded?
Nay, ye do wrong, and defraud, and that
your brethren.**

We've watched other Christians who have resolved
differences outside of court by going to church leadership with a heart of humility and a desire for God's will
in their relationships with others. Remember, in the long
run, whatever a person attempts to get out of a wrong
heart motive will be lost. What a blessing it is not to have
strife in our hearts toward others or fear of others. What
a joy to know God is able to work in our behalf as we
allow Him to work in us and work out of us anything that
needs to be worked out.

This is abundant life, to know Him and to let Him
lead our lives. When we submit to the whole counsel of
God's Word, we agree with
God. Amos 3:3 says, **"Can
two walk together, except
they be agreed?"** Are you
walking together with Him, or
have you left Him behind as
you are walking by your own
thoughts without realizing it?
Submit to His written Word
and to His voice speaking on
the inside of your heart so that

> *Remember, in
the long run,
whatever a
person
attempts to get
out of a wrong
heart motive
will be lost.*

you are really submitting to Him and not just mentally agreeing to being submitted to God.

Sometimes there are people who say they're submitted to God but they do not submit to man. This brings us to the next area of submission.

> *In order for a person not to become deceived in submitting to just any person who claims to be a leader, there are scriptural guidelines.*

Third, Submit to Church Leadership

God ordains leadership and they must submit to Him as they lead others. But they cannot lead someone who will not submit to follow their leadership.

Hebrews 13:17 says:

Obey them that have the rule over you, and submit yourselves: for they watch for your souls, as they that must give account, that they may do it with joy, and not with grief: for that is unprofitable for you.

Of course, you should pray and ask God which church you are to become a part of and which pastor you are to follow.

In order for a person not to become deceived in submitting to just any person who claims to be a leader, there are scriptural guidelines. First, *God appoints people to be pastors, evangelists, teachers, apostles and prophets* (Ephesians 4:11). People don't just decide they want to be one of the five-fold ministry gifts. The Holy Spirit strongly speaks in their heart, and they cannot shake off the calling of God.

Years ago my husband and I held a revival in a small church where the pastor was still going to seminary. We asked him when he was called into the ministry. He said, "Well, it wasn't a call. I was going to become a doctor to help hurting people, but I couldn't pass the science and math courses so I decided to become a pastor." This sounds nice, but he did not understand pastoring as Scripture reveals it.

A person must be called within their hearts to pastor or else they will not lead people in God's direction. If a person doesn't hear God's direction personally on their calling in life, how can they hear His direction for other people?

Matthew 7:20 says, **"Wherefore by their fruits ye shall know them."** The fruit of a pastor will come from a heart that is committed to feeding and watching over his flock. His purpose is first, to help them establish that they are truly saved, help them know what the Word of God teaches and enable them to share it with others (1 Timothy 2:4). Secondly, his purpose is to bring spiritual maturity to believers so they are built up and equipped in the knowledge and understanding of the Word of God (Ephesians 4:12). Thirdly, his purpose is to bring unity among believers in Christ (Ephesians 4:13). Fourthly, his purpose is to establish believers on the solid foundation of Scripture so they are not tossed and carried about with every wind of doctrine (Ephesians 4:14; Hebrews 13:9). Fifthly, his purpose is to speak the truth in love (Ephesians 4:15) and not be afraid to lovingly confront areas in believers' lives that need to come in line with the Word of God. Sixthly, his purpose is to teach believers to do their part in ministry within the church, and to reconcile others in the world to Jesus Christ (2 Corinthians 5:18).

First Peter 5:1-5 says the pastor and other five-fold ministry gifts who stand as elders in the church are:

> *Accountability is necessary for right-relatedness.*

1. To feed the flock.
2. To take oversight of them and to watch over them.
3. To not allow a wrong motive to gain fame and fortune.
4. To not control the lives of those around them, but instead, to lead believers by their counsel and by the example of their lives. They let people see the Word working in their lives and how they do it so they can follow.
5. To teach the younger leaders to be submissive to older leaders.

Every believer should be a submitted member of a local church body. The reason for this is that each believer must have someone watching over their soul, someone that they are accountable to as a leader.

Accountability is necessary for right-relatedness. Many people want to attend a church meeting once a week to salve their conscience, but they do not want anyone to know them well enough to correct them or bring them to face responsibility for their wrong attitudes or actions. This is why within the church there are sins that go on like people who commit the same sins in the world. This is also why the world has criticized and mocked the church.

Some have left churches when they felt someone in leadership knew about their wrong lifestyles, only to go where no one would know them so they could continue as they were in hidden sin. Ultimately, this deception will bring a payday, however. The result will be hurt and broken lives.

The day of living "under cover" is over. God is requiring His people to walk out of the darkness into the light. This can only begin through allowing church leadership to lead you and hold you accountable to Jesus and to others around you. If Jesus had to submit, how much more should we? This brings us to our next area of submission.

Fourth, Submit One to Another in the Fear of the Lord

In Ephesians, chapter 5, Paul was writing to the church of Ephesus (and to us) that we, as Christians, are to walk in the light and not in darkness (vv. 5-20), understanding the evil days we live in and what the will of the Lord is for our lives.

He tells us to walk in the light by being filled with the Holy Spirit, by speaking the Word of God to ourselves and by praising God. He then concludes this portion to believers by saying, **"Submitting yourselves one to another in the fear of God"** (v. 21). Why did he include this statement? I believe it was because he knew that every person needs to humble themselves and allow the input of others in their lives. No one is an island to himself. No one person has all the answers and is so self-sufficient that they do not need other people around them to help them grow in the Lord.

Promise Keepers is an international men's ministry organization that God is using everywhere to cross denominational and racial boundaries. They are bringing men into accountability and responsibility as leaders in their homes and in the church, submitted under their pastors.

This powerful ministry has a principle that every believer should live by. The principle is that every person needs (1) a Paul, (2) a Barnabas, and (3) a Timothy. Paul represents the spiritual leader (such as your pastor) who speaks into your life on a weekly basis and calls you to responsibility for your life. Barnabas represents a Christian friend who knows you better than others know you, who can speak encouragement, correction and counsel into your life, as well as pray with you when you need prayer. Timothy represents someone who has just been saved or is young in the Lord and needs help growing as a Christian.

Having these three types of people in our lives holds us accountable and responsible for our actions and attitudes. Hebrews 13:16 says, **"But to do good and to communicate forget not: for with such sacrifices God is well pleased."** The word *communicate* in the Greek is "koinonia." W. E. Vine says that the literal translation here is to "be not forgetful of good deed and of fellowship (koinonia). See *communion.*"[2] Webster defines *fellowship* as "mutual sharing as of experience, activity, interest, etc." He defines *communion* as "the act of sharing one's thoughts and emotions with one another or others; an intimate relationship with deep understanding."[3] The word *fellowship* in today's society has a surface level connotation to it, but the word *communion* has a much stronger exhortation to us.

I believe Paul, in his letter of Hebrews 13, verse 16, meant that we need other Christian brothers and/or sisters around us, in a communion level of friendship, to help us in our Christian walk.

One minister once said that "koinonia" is an "in your

---

[2]   *Vine, W. E. An Expository Dictionary of New Testament Words*, Nashville, TN: Thomas Nelson, Publishers, p. 206.
[3]   *Webster's New World Dictionary, Op. Cit.,* pp. 287,514.

face relationship." Obviously, you will not have opportunity to have this type of relationship with everyone in a church, but you should with at least one or more who can speak into your life where you won't walk away offended. We all need someone who knows us so well that they can be totally honest and open with us and we with them. We all need people who we can talk to about difficult matters with loving confrontation when needed.

First Peter 5:5 says, **"...Yea, all of you be subject one to another, and be clothed with humility: for God resisteth the proud, and giveth grace to the humble."** Pride is the one reason some Christians never allow anyone to get this close to them. Submission and koinonia fellowship require humility. Some never become a connected part of the Body of Christ because their pride never lets them connect.

Some feel no one in the church can be trusted, when in reality, they are using this criticism to cover their own shortcomings. Believe me, we all know that the church is full of imperfect people and sometimes people disappoint people. However, a truly surrendered Christian always realizes their own shortcomings and knows better than to judge the whole church because their judgment will come back on them in a stricter judgment (James 2:12-13).

The scripture does say in 1 Corinthians 11:31 NASB, **"But if we judged ourselves rightly, we should not be judged."** If a believer does not judge himself (herself), he (she) will be judged. Sin has its own judgment and can come in different ways. Some lose marriages. Some lose good health. Some lose their lives. I would rather have a friend confront me in the love of Jesus so I could avoid calamity or unnecessary problems if I could not see trouble coming.

Not becoming connected with others basically boils down to pride. Pride causes a person to feel sufficient within themselves. One day, however, pride will cause a fall or it will create a situation that is so overwhelming you have to call on or receive from the very ones you rejected. Pride isn't worth holding on to. It has the potential to destroy a person. Humble yourself and allow others in your life.

Submission in the Home

Why do children and youth have problems today submitting to governmental authority or authorities at church or school? If they never see it by example in their homes and in their parents' attitudes toward governmental, church and school authorities, then they never learn to walk in it themselves. Their attitudes are formed by the people around them, especially those they live with.

Paul writes in Ephesians 5:22-33 that wives are to submit to their own husbands, *as unto the Lord.* (Note: "As unto the Lord" releases us from submitting to anything that is immoral, abusive or against God's principles.)

If you are a wife, how do you submit to the Lord? Do you do it grudgingly? Do you resent the Lord's leadership in your life? Do you do what you want to do and call it the Lord's leading? If you are in a marriage relationship, do you, as a wife, yield to your husband's leadership by going through the motions of it but resent his leadership in your heart? God knows and people know when your heart is not into what you do. As a Christian wife, you will desire to love your husband, show him respect and help him with the things he needs. (Again, let me reiterate, I'm not referring to an abusive relationship.)

If you are a husband, do you submit yourself to God in humility? Or do you do what you want to do and then call it God's leading? Do you do for your wife and children what will benefit them, or do you do what will benefit yourself only? If you truly love your wife as Christ loves the church, you'll continually lay down your life for her. Your own selfish desires and opinions will become flexible in order to meet your wife's and children's needs and do what is best for everyone. You will love them in spite of and not because of what they do or don't do. You will want to lead them to a church where they can be spiritually nourished. You will pray for them on your own and speak God's Word in prayer for them. You will cherish them and care for them.

With these kinds of parents, it makes it much easier for children to learn submission.

Ephesians 6:1-3 goes on to say, **"Children, obey** [or submit to] **your parents** *in the Lord*: **for this is right. Honour** [give respect to] **thy father and mother; which is the first commandment with promise; that it may be well with thee, and thou mayest** *live long on the earth.*" (Note: "In the Lord" releases us from submitting to anything that would be immoral, physically or sexually abusive, or against God's principles.)

This is a command, not a suggestion. If obeyed, it has a promise of well-being and long life. It is followed by an instruction *to the leader, the father,* to **"...provoke not your children to wrath..."** (v. 4). *To provoke* means "not to joke with cutdowns, irritate, be inconsistent with your demands on them while your own life is undisciplined and slack, or purposefully make them resent you." *Wrath* means "turbulent passions and rage," according to Dake. He goes on to say, "Avoid severity, anger, harshness, cruelty. Cruel parents generally have bad children. Correct and discipline, but do not punish. *Punishment* is from a principle of revenge; *correction* is from a principle of affectionate concern."*

Why do some youth desire to hurt their parents and other people today? Could it be that some have been driven by rage because of the parents themselves? This is not always the case, but there are some in this category. Proverbs 11:29 TLB says, **"The fool who provokes his family to anger and resentment will finally have nothing worthwhile left...."**

Ephesians 6:4 says, **"...but bring them up in the nurture** [training, education, discipline and loving correction] **and admonition of the Lord** [warning through teaching and caution against harm]."

This is divine order in the home. *Some have abused these scriptures and used them as a weapon against one another instead of as a loving, God-given plan for an abundant home life.* Whenever these scriptures are abused, it is always because of *selfishness* and *pride*. First Corinthians 13:5 NIV says love **"...is not self-seeking...."** This verse in *The Living Bible* says that love **"...does not demand its own way...."** Proverbs 13:10 says, **"Only by pride cometh** *contention* [or *strife*]...." Proverbs 11:2 says, **"When pride cometh, then cometh shame...."** When a Christian home is broken up and the sense of shame comes, repent of *selfishness* and *pride*. Then let God restore. Proverbs 11:9 TLB says, **"Evil words destroy.**

---

* Dake, Finis Jennings. *The Dake Annotated Reference Bible*, Lawrenceville, GA: Dake Bible Sales, Inc., 1963, 1991, pp. 207, 212.

Godly skill rebuilds." God can show you step by step how to rebuild what you've broken down if you ask Him, listen to Him and obey Him.

Submission (or yieldedness and willingness to adjust) in Ephesians 5:21 can be carried over into the home as well as into the church. It takes a humble spirit to be willing to yield and listen to the suggestions of others around you as possible insight from the Lord. God at times can use others to bring helpful insight to accomplish something or to help you avoid a pitfall that you might not see on your own.

Offense

The next area God began showing me that some Christians could become deceived in is *offense.* Jesus said, **"...It is impossible but that *offences* will come..."** (Luke 17:1). This is a promise we don't even have to believe for. It will happen.

Verses 3 and 4 of this same chapter from *The New International Version* of the Bible say:

> **So watch yourselves. If your brother sins, rebuke him, and if he repents, forgive him. If he sins against you seven times in a day, and seven times comes back to you and says, "I repent," forgive him.**

Many people get saved and think that every Christian will act like Jesus all the time. That's impossible because we are all at different spiritual levels of growth in Him. We are called to be like Jesus Who has come to live inside of us. However, we are still in a war of the Spirit against the flesh (Galatians 5:17).

Some who have had more time to grow in the Lord have learned to be sensitive to the Holy Spirit and to others around them. They've learned how to bring their bodies under submission to the Word of God. Others are still very immature spiritually. They are self-centered, insensitive to others and haven't yet learned to yield to the voice of the Holy Spirit.

Then there are some who were saved years before but never renewed their minds to the Word of God, so for years they sit in churches and become thorns in the flesh to other Christians. Like thorns on a rose, they prick people and hurt others around them who are trying to be like the rose (Jesus). It has been said that some scientists believe the thorns on a rose are actually unde-

> *We are called to be like Jesus Who has come to live inside of us.*

veloped rosebuds. A parallel to that is, there are many undeveloped Christians pricking others around them as well as developed Christians who are like the rosebud, blessing others with their lives for Christ.

The point that I am making is that Christians will have the opportunity to become offended at some time in their lives by other Christians as well as by those without Christ. Don't let yourself take the offense and become bitter toward the church and all Christians. I've seen this through the years. Some Christians get offended and then say, "The Church kills its wounded." If you keep saying this often enough, you will believe it, quit the church and ultimately lose your relationship with God. Let offense go! Don't give the devil an opportunity with your words.

Remember, Jesus did not get offended, even at the cursing of people and the rejection of His own disciples. The temple leadership of that day continually offended

Him, but He never harbored their offenses. He gave Nicodemus mercy when He came to him. There were others who had troubled Him who later received Him. He would not have been able to receive them if He had held offense in His heart toward them. He could have said, "The Church kills its wounded." He knew better than this.

> *Although attitudes may need to be adjusted in some people over the way they treat those in sin, the message of God's Word cannot be adjusted to soothe the conscience of those in sin.*

He realized the enemy behind all evil. People were not His enemies, but the unseen realm was where His enemy dwelt. He went to the cross, and as He died He said, **"Father, forgive them; for they know not what they do"** (Luke 23:34).

Sometimes Christians are offended by the message of the Gospel, because it hits them where it hurts and they must face responsibility for the Word they've heard. In Matthew 14 Herodias was offended by John the Baptist speaking truth regarding her and King Herod's sin of adultery. In Matthew 12 the Pharisees were offended by Jesus and His disciples healing a man and casting the devil out of another man.

Today, there are some people who are offended at the Word of God regarding homosexuality. Our salvation is more important than holding on to a lifestyle that is based on pride and the lust of the flesh. Although attitudes may need to be adjusted in some people over the way they treat those in sin, the message of God's Word cannot be adjusted to soothe the conscience of those in sin.

The important factor is to know what to do with offense. If it is by the preaching of the Gospel that someone is offended, they must let go of pride, humble themselves, repent, ask forgiveness, change and bring forth fruits of repentance in their lives. If the offense is because of someone hurting you, you must choose to forgive. Holding offense will become bitterness, and bitterness will defile you and others. In the end, it will keep you out of heaven (see Hebrews 12:14-15, Mark 11:25, and Matthew 6:12). Offense is a device of Satan (2 Corinthians 2:11). Don't give him any place (Ephesians 4:27). Release it and let it go.

If you feel you need to speak to the person who has offended you in order to correct something, first get rid of anything wrong in your own heart so that when you go to them you can see clearly how to confront them lovingly (Matthew 7:1-5). Then Matthew 18:15-17 says to go to your Christian brother or sister and tell them privately. (Note: Go in an attitude of meekness and gentleness and do not strive, 2 Timothy 2:24-26.) If they receive your words, you've gained back your friendship. If they don't receive your words, go again to them with another Christian brother or sister with the same attitude of 2 Timothy 2:24-26. If they still don't receive you, then go to the church leadership and share it with them in order that they may go with you to the brother or sister and speak to them again with the same attitude of 2 Timothy 2:24-26. (Note: This Scripture doesn't mean for every offense of this kind to be brought before the whole church body. Otherwise, churches would never be able to have worship services because of reconciling multitudes of offenses. It is to be taken before the "church leadership.")

If the person still does not receive them, scripture says to treat them as a heathen (a non-Christian). The church doesn't shun a non-Christian, but understands they don't know what they are doing. There's no close fellowship or communion with someone who stubbornly goes their own way because they won't receive help. Dake says, "Be a Christian toward him as you would a stranger whom you would seek to win to Christ."[5]

I've heard some people say, "I've forgiven but I can't forget." Jesus commands us to forgive. Then we choose to release from our minds the negative thoughts of past offenses in order to go forward. It doesn't mean we can't remember anything that happened. It means that when we look back on incidents, we are no longer holding hurt and resentment toward people. Instead, we see the victory through Jesus over the offense. We are able to love the very ones who offended us through God's grace. God then uses what the enemy intended to destroy us with and turns it to help others overcome.

Isaiah 43:18-19 says:

Remember ye not the former things, neither consider the things of old.

Behold, I will do a new thing; now it shall spring forth; shall ye not know it? I will even make a way in the wilderness, and rivers in the desert.

God can make a way for us to go forward with our lives when we release the past. The river of His Spirit can renew us and restore us to go on with the Lord.

---

[5]   Ibid., New Testament p. 20.

Forgiveness isn't based on feelings but on *faith.*
Sometimes it is an act of faith to forgive another person.
There are times that God will require you to prove your
forgiveness by an act of kindness toward the one you've
forgiven. This helps seal your forgiveness. When you forgive, ask God to remove the
"sting" of the hurt from you.

> *When you forgive,
> ask God to remove
> the "sting" of the
> hurt from you.*

Remember how Jesus
defeated death and the grave.
Even though people still go
through death and the grave,
Jesus took the sting out of death and the victory out of
the grave (1 Corinthians 15:54-55). When we forgive and
ask for God to remove the "sting" of the offense, we have
the victory over the offense instead of the offense having
victory over us. Later on, as we look back on the offense,
it isn't a "bitter pill," but it is a "sweet triumph" in Christ
in order to help others that we witness to, to overcome
their offenses also.

Become Involved in Your Local Church

The next area of right-relatedness that God spoke in
my heart was in Ephesians 4:16. There are many "floaters"
in the Body of Christ who never get into one local church
and stay there to grow. If you take a plant and uproot it
every month, it will not grow. It has to be planted and
allowed to take root in one place in order to grow and bear
fruit or flower.

Ephesians 4:14 says, **"That we henceforth be no
more children** [never growing up], **tossed to and fro,
and carried about with every wind of doctrine..."** but
we're to be as verse 16 says **"...fitly joined together and

compacted [in the Greek, *compacted* means "to be united or knit together"] **by that which every joint supplieth, according to the effectual working in the measure of every part, maketh increase of the body unto the edifying of itself in love."** In other words, each part works properly, causing growth for the Body and building itself up in love.

If a believer never becomes an active member in a local body but simply remains a spectator each week, there is no relationship happening with others. As a result, they are not growing. This person may be gaining head knowledge, but his or her character and life are not being developed because it takes relating to people with the help of God's Word, for a person to mature.

For example, it's easy to be patient, peaceful, or joyful when it's just you and God alone. However, the foundation and commission of Christianity are to reach and disciple others. People will press you, and your response to that pressure will determine your spiritual growth.

Once we have prayed and asked God which local church we are to become a member of, we should ask the Lord what our part or function is that we're called to do in that body of believers. God will put in your heart a desire to help in some area. For example, if you enjoy working with children, then possibly you are to help teach or be an assistant in the nursery. If you enjoy serving people and preparing things, then possibly you are called to help set up the rooms and organize materials for others to use. Or, if you are a person who loves to meet people, maybe you are called to greet and welcome people at the door.

Whatever your interests are, God will use those interests to meet a need in the local body of believers you become a part of. Every person is needed in every church. Never compare yourself with someone else and forfeit functioning in the role you are called to function in. As one minister has said, "Find a need and meet it; find a hurt and heal it." Whatever you do to help within the local body of believers, do it with all your heart as unto the Lord, not as unto men. Then you'll receive His rewards. People who do anything out of a wrong motive of heart will become disappointed and hurt in the long run. When you do what you do as unto the Lord, you'll always have peaceful contentment that He sees and knows (Colossians 3:23-24).

We are living in a day where many people appear all together on the outside but are hurting on the inside. We should not think that people who go to church never have hurts or needs. The church is a place of healing, restoring, training, sending and encouraging.

Hebrews 10:24-25 says:

And let us consider one another to provoke unto love and to good works:

Not forsaking the assembling of ourselves together, as the manner of some is; but exhorting one another: and so much the more, as ye see the day approaching.

The word *consider* means "to discover and behold one another." Many Christians go to church for years and never discover the testimonies and giftings in those around them because they are self-centered, afraid to get to know others, or so busy living their own lives they never take time to know someone else. Take time to "discover" those around you.

Then the writer of Hebrews says we are to provoke one another unto love and good works. Some people need urging. The word *provoke*, "paroxusmos" in Greek, means "to urge, prick, irritate and excite; to make keen."[6] A comparison would be that of an oyster getting a grain of sand inside of it. The grain of sand irritates the oyster. The oyster releases a substance that covers the grain of sand with many layers until a smooth round pearl is formed.

> *If you allow God to use people to help you grow, you'll become a precious gem in the Body of Christ.*

You may feel like some Christians provoke or irritate you a lot. Realize, this irritation is forcing you to grow in your love walk. Then, on the other hand, some Christians provoke by exciting you to do more for the Kingdom of God. You need both. If you allow God to use people to help you grow, you'll become a precious gem in the Body of Christ.

Verse 25 of Hebrews 10 goes on to say, don't stop gathering together as a group of believers on a regular basis like some Christians have. Instead, congregate more and more so that you can exhort one another to faithfulness as you see the day of Jesus' return drawing near. Do you realize how close we are to His coming? All those in Christian leadership are speaking of the signs of these end times drawing to a close. Even scientists realize the world is showing signs of the earth moving toward an end. Some people have even had angelic visitations speaking of the return of Jesus being very soon. According to the scrip-

---

[6] Ibid., p. 252.

ture, Christians need to meet together more and more and not stop going to church gatherings. We need each other to be strong for these days.

Valuing *Every Member* of the Body of Christ

We need each other in the *entire* Body of Christ. This is no time for building walls and excluding one another in the Christian faith. The church and five-fold ministry gifts — apostles, prophets, evangelists, pastors and teachers (Ephesians 4:11) — who are preaching that Jesus Christ is the answer and the way to eternal life, need each other. Methodists, Baptists, Pentecostals, Episcopalians, Presbyterians, Charismatics, and others who preach salvation through Jesus Christ alone must not criticize one another, but instead, appreciate one another. We are working *together* to build the Kingdom of Jesus Christ and win souls.

Racial Reconciliation

The Holy Spirit spoke within my heart that God is going to require Christians and churches who truly want His Kingdom to come and His will to be done, to drop racial walls of prejudice. We must become sensitive to the hurts and offenses of one another to bring healing and reconciliation. God is not black, white, brown, or beige. He comprises every color and facial makeup of all people everywhere, because we as humans are all made in His image. We have all come out of Him. He is Father to all who will accept Him as Creator and His Son as Lord and Savior.

I heard a minister recently quote from John 17:21,

> *We must become sensitive to the hurts and offenses of one another to bring healing and reconciliation.*

"Jesus prayed that His disciples (or Christians) would become one, even as He and the Father are one so the world would believe." Then he added, "Jesus always gets His prayers answered!"

We must begin to reach out beyond our comfort zones and include others who may seem different than we are. As another minister has said, "We must enlarge our circle of love," not only racially, but socially, economically and physically. We must reach out to include people from all walks of life. The rich, the poor, the handicapped, the down-and-outers, the up-and-outers, the prostitute, the business person, the drug addict, the biker, the trucker, the cowboy, those with long hair, short hair, earrings, nose rings, those wearing jeans, dresses, etc.

The church that will become a mixture of all people who need Jesus and need discipling, restoring and freeing will be alive. Those who resist this will become simply a form of dead religion with living bodies but no life that sets people free. Jesus is not religion. He is life. The church that reaches out to all people groups is alive because lives are continually being transformed, and then these new converts are bringing others in to be transformed by Jesus.

> *The bond that knits all of these people together is agape, or the God-kind of love. It is a love in spite of, not because of.*

The bond that knits all of these people together is agape, or the God-kind of love. It is a love in spite of, not because of. It is a love that is giving and seeks to benefit others. It is a love that is pure and unconditional. It is a love that reaches out beyond itself.

The church that will hear and obey what the Spirit of God is saying in this hour will become more and more like what Jesus has desired it to be.

GIVING OUT OF YOURSELF

*T*he last area that God began showing me how some Christians either have been or could become deceived in, is the area of giving out of themselves. He spoke to me that it was not *just* witnessing, or *just* giving of our money to God. But it also involves laying our lives down totally to Jesus in order to share with others what we have received. It becomes a lifestyle of sharing love and whatever Jesus tells us to share.

Growing up as a child, I remember visiting my grandparents' home in Arkansas. They lived on the edge of town where my grandfather owned some land around his little house and raised a few cattle. Although his main job was working at the local lumbermill as a foreman, he enjoyed his cows.

There were two ponds on the property, so each time we visited, my brother and I would walk to the ponds and then hike around the property. One pond had a small creek that fed into it, but it had no outlet. It was stagnant. There was green slime covering a large portion of the pond's surface and there were snakes in the water along with some fish. The cows would congregate around it to drink and wade out into it. I remember thinking how gross it was seeing the green slime dripping off of their mouths and bodies. I was very cautious of snakes at the water's edge whenever I would go around it. I knew better than to swim in that pond.

The other pond was up a hill nestled in the midst of several beautiful pine trees. There was a creek flowing in it and a creek flowing out of it. It was so clear you could see the small fish swimming around in the water. Most of the time we waded in it, but we would also sit back and just admire it as we talked.

The difference in the two ponds is like the difference in some Christians. The Christian who always takes in and never gives out is like the stagnant pond. I've known youth and adults who are so accustomed to hearing the latest speaker or singer who has a little different approach and comes to make them feel good or gives them one more revelation, yet not be changed. Instead, some become dull of hearing and some even develop hardness of heart.

Hebrews 5:11-14 NASB says:

Concerning him [Jesus] **we have much to say, and it is hard to explain, since you have become dull of hearing.**

For though by this time you ought to be teachers, you have need again for someone to teach you the elementary principles of the oracles of God, and you have come to need milk and not solid food.

For everyone who partakes only of milk is not accustomed to the word of righteousness, for he is a babe.

But solid food is for the mature, who because of practice have their senses trained to discern good and evil.

Paul says you are dull of hearing and can't receive. I've noticed when people sit week after week and take in

> *I've found the
> more I share Jesus
> with people, the
> more I grow in
> discernment and
> sensitivity.*

messages but never give out, they become *dull of hearing.* They make comments like, "Oh, yeah, I've heard that speaker or that subject taught on before." They become critical and quick to judge others. They feel they know enough that they could coast on what they know until they die. They are *dull* spiritually. You can't tell them anything else, because they can't relate to it since they aren't using what they have learned.

In the natural realm, people who never exercise or move their bodies around to work off what they've eaten at meals will become "fat and sassy." They can talk about all the latest foods and restaurants, but they also become very critical. They can even get tired of what they have. Those who exercise and work hard are always hungry at mealtime and are usually grateful for what they get.

I've found the more I give out, the more I need to take in each time I'm at a church service. Jesus said in John 4:34, His meat (or solid food) was to *do* the will of Him Who sent Him. Some think the meat of God's Word is some deep teaching. No! The meat is doing what you've been taught, then you will see deeper truths about the very Word of God you are doing.

Jesus' meat in John 4 was leading a woman in sin to living water. I've found the more I share Jesus with people, the more I grow in discernment and sensitivity. Hebrews 5:14 says, **"But strong meat belongeth to them that are of full age, even those who by reason of use have their senses exercised to discern both good**

and evil." In other words, by using the Word as we share it with others, we discern good and evil. We become sharper in discerning people in order to better minister to them as well. I've also discovered greater understanding of the Scripture as I share it with others.

If you take in all the time and never give out, you sense no responsibility for people around you. You have an attitude that your life is your own and you should be able to do whatever you want whether it affects someone else negatively or not. Romans 14:7 NASB says, **"For not one of us lives for himself, and not one dies for himself."** Someone who lives for himself or herself becomes self-centered. This person doesn't do anything unless there's something in it for him or her. Normally, this person is also critical of others who at least are trying to do something for the Kingdom of God. This critical spirit is like the snakes in my grandparents' pond which I spoke of earlier, who are poisonous and will bite.

Paul wrote the church at Philippi that he was short on committed workers like Timothy. He said in Philippians 2:20-21:

> **For I have no man likeminded** [who wanted to reach out and help others like himself and Timothy], **who will naturally care for your state.**
>
> **For all** *seek their own, not the things which are Jesus Christ's.*

Webster defines *selfishness* as "too much concern with one's own welfare or interests and having little or no concern for others; self-centered; showing or prompted by self-interest."[1] He defines *selflessness* (the opposite of selfishness

---

[1] *Webster's New World Dictionary*, New York, NY: Simon & Schuster, 1982, p. 1292.

and egoism) as "devoted to others' welfare or interests and not one's own; unselfish; altruistic; self-sacrificing."[2] *Altruism* is defined the same as *selflessness*, plus, "the doctrine that the general welfare of society is the proper goal of an individual's action, as opposed to *egoism.*"[3] Webster defines *egoism* as "to be self-centered or to consider only oneself and one's own interests; selfishness; egotism; conceit; the doctrine that self-interest is the proper goal of all human actions; opposed to *altruism.*"[4]

If the Body of Christ only had self-centered Christians, Christianity would never spread to the world but would ultimately die. This isn't the Christian life that the New Testament teaches. Jesus said to His disciples in Matthew 10:8, **"...freely ye have received, freely give."** As Christians we've all received the gift of salvation, forgiveness, freedom, healing, restoration and more by God's grace. It is now our calling, responsibility and commission as believers to give out to others the truths we have received so they can escape hell, make heaven and experience all Jesus wants to do in their lives now.

The clear pond that had a flow of water going in and then a flow of water going out represents the Christian who receives in order to give. Their motives are pure as they share the Gospel with others. They care about others. They are not caught up with just living life to benefit themselves. They care about others' souls.

My husband has shared an illustration that bears repeating. Suppose that a bridge is out and it is nighttime. In the midst of a heavy rainstorm, you discover that the

---

[2]   Ibid.
[3]   Ibid., p. 41.
[4]   Ibid., p. 446.

133

bridge is out just before arriving at it. You can see car lights approaching from a distance. Would you get your flashlight out and begin to wave it in order to stop them from plunging off of the bridge into the deep, raging waters?

There are multitudes plunging into darkness and hell. Some are even backslidden Christians plunging into sin and its web of destruction. Some are Christians who never got the Word of God strong enough in them who are becoming deceived by wrong relationships, cults, the lust for money and power, etc. Who will stop them and help them?

Second Corinthians 5:11 NIV says:

Since, then, we know what it is to fear the Lord, we try to persuade men. What we are is plain to God, and I hope it is also plain to your conscience.

Verses 18 and 19 of 2 Corinthians 5 NIV tell us that God has given us the ministry and calling of reconciliation. He was in Christ reconciling the world to Himself, and now He is in us so we can reconcile people to Him.

All this is from God, who reconciled us to himself through Christ and gave us the ministry of reconciliation:

That God was reconciling the world to himself in Christ, not counting men's sins against them. And he has committed to us the message of reconciliation.

The last words Jesus said were for us to go make disciples in all nations (or in all people groups). Then He said we (as Christians) are to be involved in teaching others to observe or obey all that He has commanded us in

His written Word. (See Matthew 28:18-20.) This Great Commission is not just for preachers, it is for all believers. *It is not a suggestion, but a command.* Every born-again Christian is to have a heart for people who do not know Jesus personally or do not have knowledge of the Word to walk free. It is having the heart of God for people.

There are times people have come to me and said, "I'm just waiting on my calling." Usually they have been waiting for a couple of years or so. This may be an awakening, *but why are you waiting?* The call has been given by Jesus. The Great Commission is to go and share this Gospel with others and teach them His commands. Don't wait for someone to recognize your abilities. Just find a need and start meeting it. Needs are everywhere.

> *This Great Commission is not just for preachers, it is for all believers. It is not a suggestion, but a command.*

John 15:16 says He has ordained you to go and bring forth fruit. **"Ye have not chosen me, but I have chosen you, and ordained you, that ye should go and bring forth fruit...."** There are jails and prisons, juvenile delinquent centers, nursing homes, women's and men's shelters, hospitals and other avenues of outreach. If a person begins to find a need and meet it, others will notice. No ministry wants to hire someone who is sitting back doing nothing and waiting to be called. Start doing something. *You cannot steer or direct a car that is not in motion.*

Acts 1:8 NASB says:

> **But you shall receive power when the Holy Spirit has come upon you; and you shall be My**

**witnesses both in Jerusalem, and in all Judea
and Samaria, and even to the remotest part of
the earth.**

The reason for this "clothing upon" or "endowment of
power from on high" as Luke 24:49 says regarding Jesus'
prophecy of the Holy Spirit coming upon believers, is to
empower us to be His witnesses. Not just witnessing
words but also the demonstration of the Gospel we preach
through signs and wonders by believing and praying in
God's power through Jesus' name. (See Romans 15:18-
19, Mark 16:15-20 and the entire book of Acts.)

I've had numerous times where I've been on an ele-
vator, at a gas station, seated on an airplane, or in another place, and began witnessing to someone who needed
prayer for healing or counsel. After praying, they would
say to me, in shock, "I feel better." Then they were ready
to pray the sinner's prayer with me right at that moment.
Other times, I've gotten right to the point of praying for
their salvation quickly. It only takes two or three minutes
to have someone pray the sinner's prayer with you.

Time is short. It's time to become lovingly bold!
People are touched if they know you really care for them
and you're not just witnessing to earn brownie points
with God. Sometimes you may have
time to sit and listen and answer
questions to convince them to accept
Jesus. At other times, you may not
have as much time. Sometimes people are ripe for harvest. At other
times, they may be "smug." Don't let
rejection stop you. Witness to someone else.

> *Time is short. It's time to become lovingly bold!*

After praying the sinner's prayer with people, always instruct them to read the Bible daily, starting in the New Testament. Then instruct them to pray daily and go to a church that is alive. Finally, encourage them to tell someone else what has happened to them.

Jesus knew that it wasn't enough to get people to accept Him as their Savior, but that they must also be instructed on living a new life in Him (Matthew 28:20). As we help others who are coming into the Kingdom, we will have to bear with them in their growth process.

Romans 15:1-7 NIV says:

We who are strong ought to bear with the failings of the weak *and not to please ourselves*. Each of us should please his neighbor for his good, to build him up. For even Christ did not please himself but, as it is written: "The insults of those who insult you have fallen on me." For everything that was written in the past was written to teach us, so that through endurance and the encouragement of the Scriptures we might have hope.

May the God who gives endurance and encouragement give you a spirit of unity among yourselves as you follow Christ Jesus, so that with one heart and mouth you may glorify the God and Father of our Lord Jesus Christ.

Accept one another, then, just as Christ accepted you, in order to bring praise to God.

In giving out of our lives, we become yielded to God for Him to make us sensitive to see a need and meet it. Some Christians have no sensitivity because they live their lives for themselves. They may be seemingly good

137

people but do not want to be
bothered with anything other
than the things that benefit their
lives.

> *Insensitivity has been a hindrance or a "sore" in the Body of Christ for years.*

Insensitivity of a church's
members is why some people,
who are down and out, go to a
church and sometimes get hurt
and offended. As long as new people look similar to
them, the members of that congregation accept them.
However, if they appear too obviously different, there is
a feeling that comes across that says, "You don't really fit
here, so go someplace else. We will not miss you."
Insensitivity has been a hindrance or a "sore" in the Body
of Christ for years. It takes a deliberate choice to become
sensitive and reach out to others beyond our family, our
group, our race, or our comfort zone. It is a part of giving out of yourself.

Philippians 2:3-14 TLB says:

**Don't be selfish; don't live to make a good
impression on others. Be humble, thinking of
others as better than yourself. Don't just think
about your own affairs, but be interested in others, too, and in what they are doing.**

**Your attitude should be the kind that was
shown us by Jesus Christ, who, though he was
God, did not demand and cling to his rights as
God, but laid aside his mighty power and glory,
taking the disguise of a slave and becoming like
men. And he humbled himself even further,
going so far as actually to die a criminal's death
on a cross.**

Yet it was because of this that God raised him up to the heights of heaven and gave him a name which is above every other name, that at the name of Jesus every knee shall bow in heaven and on earth and under the earth, and every tongue shall confess that Jesus Christ is Lord, to the glory of God the Father.

Dearest friends, when I was there with you, you were always so careful to follow my instructions. And now that I am away you must be even more careful to do the good things that result from being saved, obeying God with deep reverence, shrinking back from all that might displease him. For God is at work within you, helping you want to obey him, and then helping you do what he wants.

In everything you do, stay away from complaining and arguing.

I shared in the previous chapter on the principle of Promise Keepers, that everyone needs a Paul (a spiritual elder teaching them and holding them accountable); a Barnabas (a spiritual brother or sister who can speak into their life as a friend and hold them accountable); and a Timothy (a younger Christian to disciple and be responsible for). You may feel you have several "Timothys" that you have a friendship relationship with and who you are helping to grow in the Lord. It keeps you living responsibly. It makes you feel fulfilled as you see them grow. It strengthens and encourages you. This principle will keep you alive and healthy spiritually.

Since being in ministry for twenty-four years, may I share a note of guidance for working one on one with individuals? If you are a female, work with a female; and if you are a male, work with a male. If you are a married couple, then together you can work with males or females in discipling. If you teach a mixed singles group, have someone of the opposite sex help you disciple those of the opposite sex. This guideline has helped to avoid emotional entanglements in relationships that needed to be kept as friendships and not bring regrets later.

Another way of giving out of ourselves is in serving. Jesus said in Mark 10:42-45:

Ye know that they which are accounted to rule over the Gentiles exercise lordship over them; and their great ones exercise authority upon them.

But so shall it not be among you: but whosoever will be great among you, shall be your minister:

And whosoever of you will be the chiefest, shall be *servant* of all.

For even the Son of man came not to be ministered unto, but to minister, and to give his life a ransom for many.

No matter if we are in a position of teaching or administrating, we must all keep a servant heart. Having a servant heart will keep us from being disappointed, especially as we remember we are serving the Lord as we serve people. It will also help in how others perceive us if we seek to walk with the heart of a servant.

Romans 12:4-8 shows us different giftings people function in. Not everyone is an "up front" person. Some enjoy quietly preparing the physical environment for ministry to take place. This is very good. Some have the ability to organize and instruct people what to do to make something happen. Some are creative and have writing abilities. Others are teachers. Some enjoy exhorting others, or training people to lead others to the Lord. Some enjoy counseling one on one with individuals. Some are able to

> *The time you give to serve in the Kingdom in some capacity will be rewarded by God.*

see things that are wrong and fix them. Some are able to discern better than others. There are so many opportunities in the church to serve in some capacity. The important factors are to know that you are needed and to find where you should function. Never feel a church has enough people helping so they don't need you.

In a family of twelve, if the mom and dad and one or two brothers and sisters do everything, they become overloaded, or something doesn't get done. If everyone pulls their part of the load, even if they feel it's a small part, things go smoother, more is accomplished and training is happening in all of the family to walk in responsibility. The time you give to serve in the Kingdom in some capacity will be rewarded by God. (See Colossians 3:23-24 and Hebrews 6:10.)

Sheep or Goats?

We are to live as sheep, not as goats. We are to reach out to others to whom God leads us and minister to their natural needs as well as to their spiritual needs. Jesus said, **"...Inasmuch as ye have done it unto one of the least of these my brethren, ye have done it unto me"** (Matthew 25:40). God's sheep hear His voice and obey. Goats may hear but they are known for disobedience and for doing whatever they want to do.

Jesus explains sheep and goats in Matthew 25:31-46:

When the Son of man shall come in his glory, and all the holy angels with him, then shall he sit upon the throne of his glory:

And before him shall be gathered all nations: and he shall separate them one from another, as a shepherd divideth his sheep from the goats:

And he shall set the sheep on his right hand, but the goats on the left.

Then shall the King say unto them on his right hand, Come, ye blessed of my Father, inherit the kingdom prepared for you from the foundation of the world:

For I was an hungered, and ye gave me meat: I was thirsty, and ye gave me drink: I was a stranger, and ye took me in:

Naked, and ye clothed me: I was sick, and ye visited me: I was in prison, and ye came unto me.

Then shall the righteous answer him, saying, Lord, when saw we thee an hungered, and fed thee? or thirsty, and gave thee drink?

When saw we thee a stranger, and took thee in? or naked, and clothed thee?

Or when saw we thee sick, or in prison, and came unto thee?

And the King shall answer and say unto them, Verily I say unto you, Inasmuch as ye have done it unto one of the least of these my brethren, ye have done it unto me.

Then shall he say also unto them on the left

hand, Depart from me, ye cursed, into everlasting fire, prepared for the devil and his angels:

For I was an hungered, and ye gave me no meat: I was thirsty, and ye gave me no drink:

I was a stranger, and ye took me not in: naked, and ye clothed me not: sick, and in prison, and ye visited me not.

Then shall they also answer him, saying, Lord, when saw we thee an hungered, or athirst, or a stranger, or naked, or sick, or in prison, and did not minister unto thee?

Then shall he answer them, saying, Verily I say unto you, Inasmuch as ye did it not to one of the least of these, ye did it not to me.

And these shall go away into everlasting punishment: but the righteous into life eternal.

Joy in Giving

Giving also involves your money. Some people are resentful to give. Jesus spoke about giving. He said in Luke 6:38:

Give, and it shall be given unto you; good measure, pressed down, and shaken together, and running over, shall men give into your bosom. For with the same measure that ye mete withal it shall be measured to you again.

Jesus knew that in giving, it sooner or later returns to us some way. Giving opens the door to favor with God and man. It can't be done grudgingly or we won't receive the full benefits. God wants to make His grace (favor) abound toward you so that you will always have the sufficient amount of whatever you need in life (2 Corinthians

9:6-8). His Word also says as you give cheerfully, you will abound financially, enabling you to contribute to every good work you desire.

There is a flow of giving that many have come to understand. It produces a joy in the people who discover this flow. Malachi 3:10-11 says that as we bring our tithes and offerings to God for the work of the ministry, He opens the windows of heaven so we can be blessed, and He rebukes the devourer for our sakes. He even says that others will recognize and call us blessed as we do this. Through giving our money to Him, we are giving a part of our lives because we had to work and give our time and effort to make it. As we give it, we are saying to God that we recognize it all belongs to Him. The tithe (or the tenth) and the offerings over and above are an acknowledgement that we give Him first place (with the firstfruits) and believe for Him to direct how we spend the rest of the money. We release our faith then, believing that He supplies any extra we may need to do whatever He leads us to do.

Jesus said, **"It is more blessed to give than to receive"** (Acts 20:35). Why? Because there is a joy in giving and seeing people rejoice who have their needs met through your obedience. Then He rewards you by giving back to you through some other avenue later on.

Everywhere Jesus went He was giving. He gave His time, teaching and understanding of the Scriptures, prayer for those who desired it, healing, freedom, forgiveness, restoration, acceptance, food, etc. His life was a life of giving. Then on the cross He gave everything for you and me through His death and resurrection. If He gave us so much and continues to, how much should we give?

THE BACKSLIDER IN HEART

(When Love Grows Cold)

by
Charles G. Finney
(Edited and paraphrased from *Revival of Religion* © 1868)

The following pages are from a message of Charles Finney who warned and exhorted the people of his day. I was gripped with this message ten years ago when I first read it, and I am still challenged by it today. I pray that you'll be strengthened as you read it to recognize the symptoms of backsliding, how to avoid it and how to come out of such a state if you recognize some of the symptoms in your own life.

Sharon Daugherty

* * *

What Backsliding in Heart Is Not

It does not consist of not having exciting religious feelings. No longer having these great spiritual feelings may be an *evidence* of a backslidden heart, but it is not the *cause* of such a state.

What Backsliding in Heart Is

Backsliding in heart is:
1. Taking back that consecration to God and His service that constitutes true conversion.

2. The leaving of his/her first love by a Christian.

3. As a Christian, withdrawing yourself from entire and total surrender to God and coming again under the control of a self-pleasing spirit.

4. A person who still maintains an outward appearance of religion. We have all seen different people perform the same or similar outward acts from widely different (and often opposite) motives. No doubt the most intense selfishness often takes on a religious form. And there are many considerations that might lead a backslider in heart to keep up this spiritual show, even though he/she has lost the power of godliness in his/her soul.

What Are the Evidences of a Backslidden Heart?

Some of the *evidences* of a backslidden heart are:

1. *A lack of spiritual enjoyment.* We always love saying and doing those things that please the one we love most. When the heart is not backslidden, real communion with God is kept up, and therefore all spiritual devotions are not only performed with pleasure, but the communion with God involved in them is a source of rich and continual blessing. If we do not *enjoy* the service of God, it is because we do not truly serve Him.

2. *An outward formality in religious exercises.* A stereotyped, formal way of saying and doing things that is clearly the result of habit rather than the out-gushing of a true spiritual life. In prayer or fellowship, this formality will be emotionless and as cold as ice and will reveal a total lack of sincerity in the performance of all spiritual service. Such a state would be impossible where there is a present, living faith and a true godly zeal.

3. *An ungoverned temper.* While the heart is full of love, the temper will naturally be patient and sweet. Or if at any time it should go so far as to escape from self-control, a truly loving heart will quickly confess and break down, repenting with true humility. Whenever there is an irritable, uncontrolled temper, you may know that there is a backslidden heart.

4. *The loss of interest in truly spiritual conversation.* **"For the mouth speaks out of that which fills the heart"** (Matthew 12:34 NASB). No conversation is so sweet to a truly loving heart as that which relates to Christ and to our living Christian experience.

5. *Searching for worldly amusements.* The most grateful amusements possible to a truly spiritual mind are those that bring the soul into the most direct communion with God. A loving heart is jealous of everything that will break up or interfere with its union with God. When the soul does not find more delight in God than in all worldly things, the heart is sadly backslidden.

6. *A lack of interest in foreign missions.* If you lose your interest in these works and for reaching those in heathen lands, and do not delight in the conversion of souls everywhere, you are backslidden in heart.

7. *The loss of interest in outreaches to the poor and needy.* Surely if you were ever converted to Christ at all, you have had an interest in all charitable, Christian enterprises that came within your knowledge. A converted soul takes the deepest interest in all outreaches to reform, help and save mankind — in the provision of the needs for the poor and needy — and in short, in *every good word and work.*

8. *The loss of interest in those newly converted.*

There is joy in the presence of the angels over one sinner who repents, and is there not joy among the saints on earth over those who come to Christ and are His newly born babes in the Kingdom? Show me a professing Christian who does not have a passionate interest in converts to Christ, and I will show you a backslider in heart and a hypocrite — he professes religion, but he has none.

9. *A faultfinding, critical spirit.* The disposition to fasten blame, showing a lack of confidence in the good intentions and motives of others. It is a spirit of distrust of Christian character. It is a state of mind that reveals itself in harsh words and harsh judgments of individuals. This state is entirely incompatible with a true loving heart. Whenever a judgmental spirit is manifested by a professing Christian, you may know that there is a backslidden heart.

10. *A self-indulgent spirit.* By self-indulgence, I mean the inclination to gratify the appetites, passions and to fulfill **"...the desires of the flesh and of the mind..."** (Ephesians 2:3 NASB). The appetite for food is frequently, *and perhaps more frequently than any other*, the occasion for backsliding. Few Christians, I fear, sense any danger in this area. God's injunction is, **"Whether, then, you eat or drink or whatever you do, do all to the glory of God"** (1 Corinthians 10:31 NASB). Christians forget this and eat and drink to please themselves. More persons are ensnared by their tables than the Church is aware of. A great many people who avoid alcoholic drinks altogether will indulge in food that both in quantity and quality prove they follow no other law than that of their appetite. This indulging in gluttony threatens to

ruin both body and soul together.

11. *Absence from scheduled prayer meetings for slight reasons is a sure indication of a backslidden heart.* No meeting is more important to a Christian than the prayer meeting, and while they have any heart to pray, they will not be absent unless prevented by something urgent that God has impressed them to do. If a call from a friend at the hour of meeting can prevent their attendance, it is strong evidence that they do not really want to go. That same person visiting at such a time would not prevent them from attending a wedding, a party, a picnic, or some other enjoyable event. It is hypocrisy for them to pretend that they really want to go when they can be kept away by small excuses.

12. *The same is true of the neglect of family prayer for slight reasons.* While the heart is in love with the Lord, Christians will not readily omit a daily time of prayer and Bible reading with their family.

13. *When secret, private prayer is regarded more as a duty than as a privilege.* It has always appeared to me most ridiculous to hear Christians speak of prayer as a duty. It is an infinite privilege to be allowed to come to God and ask for the supply of all our needs. To pray because *we must* rather than because *we may* is a sad, sad thing.

14. *A lack of the spirit of prayer.* While the love of Christ remains fresh in the soul, the indwelling Spirit of God will reveal Himself as the Spirit of grace and supplication (prayer). He will instill strong desire in the soul for the salvation of sinners and the sanctification of saints. If that Spirit of prayer departs, it is a sure indication of a backslidden heart. For while the first love of a Christian continues, he is sure to be drawn by the Holy Spirit to

wrestle much in prayer.

15. *A backslidden heart often reveals itself by the manner in which people pray.* For example, praying as if in a state of condemnation, very much like an unconverted sinner, is an evidence of a backslidden heart. His confessions and self-accusations in prayer show to others what perhaps he does not well understand himself. Instead of being filled with faith and love, he is more or less convicted of sin and is conscious deep within that he is not in a state of acceptance by God.

It is often very striking and even shocking to attend a backsliders' prayer meeting, and I'm very sorry to say that many prayer meetings of the Church are little else. Their prayers are timid and hesitating and reveal the fact that they have little or no faith.

16. *The loss of interest in the question of holiness.* If you are a Christian, you have felt that sin was an abomination to your soul. You have had inexpressible longings to be rid of it forever and everything that could throw light upon that question of agonizing importance was most desperately crucial to you. If this question has been dismissed and is no longer of any interest to you, it is because you are backslidden in heart.

17. *A lack of interest in God's Word.* Perhaps nothing more conclusively proves that a Christian has a backslidden heart than losing his interest in the Bible. While the heart is full of love, no book in the world is so precious; but when the love is gone, the Bible becomes not only uninteresting, but often repulsive. There is no faith to accept its promises, but conviction enough to dread its threatenings.

The Consequences of Backsliding in Heart

1. *The backslider in heart will be filled with his own mistakes.* He is not walking with God. He is not led by the Spirit, but is walking in spiritual darkness. In this state he is sure to fall into many terrible mistakes in business, in relationships, in using his time, his tongue, his money. Indeed *all* will go wrong with him as long as he remains in a backslidden state.

2. *He shall be filled with his own feelings.* Instead of that sweet peace and rest in the Holy Spirit that he once had, he will find himself in a state of unrest, dissatisfied with himself and everyone else. It is sometimes very trying to live with a backslider. They are often touchy, faultfinding and irritating in all their ways. They have forsaken God, and in their feelings there is more of hell than of heaven.

3. *The backslider in heart will be filled with his own words.* While in this state, he *will not* and *cannot* control his tongue. It will prove itself to be an unruly member full of deadly poison (James 3:8). By his words he will entangle himself in many difficulties and problems from which he can never free himself until he comes back to God.

4. *The backslider in heart will be full of his own cares.* He has turned back to selfishness. He counts himself and his possessions as his very own and tries to manage everything for himself in his own wisdom. Consequently, his cares will be multiplied and come upon him like a deluge.

5. *The backslider in heart will be filled with his own lustings.* His appetites and passions which had been kept under control have now resumed their full course, and having been kept down so long, they will seem to avenge themselves by becoming more demanding and unruly

than ever. These animal appetites and passions will burst forth to the astonishment of the backslider, and he will probably find himself more under their control and enslaved by them than he ever was before.

6. *The backslider in heart will be full of his own troubles.* Instead of keeping out of temptation, he will run right into it. He will bring upon himself multitudes of trials. He is not at peace with God, with himself, the Church, or with the world.

7. *The backslider in heart will be filled with his own anxieties.* He will` be worried about himself — about his business, his reputation, *everything!* He has taken all these things out of the hands of God. Hence, having faith in God no longer, and being unable to control events, he is filled with worry about the future. These anxieties are the inevitable result of his madness and folly in forsaking God.

8. *The backslider in heart will be filled with his own prejudices.* His willingness to know and do the truth is gone. He will very naturally oppose any principle or truth that comes down hard on a selfish spirit. He will endeavor to justify himself. He will not want to read or hear anything which would rebuke his backslidden state, and will become deeply prejudiced against anyone who shall reprove him or correct him. Considering that person as an enemy, he will hedge himself in and shut his eyes against the light, standing on the defensive and criticizing everything that might expose him.

9. *The backslider in heart will be full of his own delusions.* Having an evil eye, his whole body will become full of darkness (Matthew 6:23). He will almost certainly fall into self-deception in regard to principles and doctrines. Wandering on in darkness as he does, he will very

likely swallow the grossest delusions. Cults of every type and deceptions of every shade may be very likely to gain possession of him.

10. *The backslider in heart must be full of his own losses.* He regards his possessions as his own, his time as his own, his influence as his own, his reputation as his own. The loss of any of these he accounts as *his own loss.* Having forsaken God, and being unable to control the events by which these things are maintained, he will find himself suffering losses on every side. He loses his peace, his property, his time and his reputation. He loses his Christian witness, and if he continues, *he loses his soul.*

11. *The backslider in heart is full of self-condemnation.* Having once enjoyed the love of God and then forsaking Him, he feels condemned for everything. If he attempts religious duty, he knows there is no heart in it, and hence condemns himself. If he neglects religious duty, he of course condemns himself. If he reads his Bible, it condemns him. If he does not read it, he feels condemned. If he goes to church meetings, the meetings condemn him. If he stays away, he feels condemned also. If he prays in secret, with his family, or at a meeting, he knows he is not sincere and is condemned. If he neglects or refuses to pray, he also feels condemned. *Everything condemns him!* His conscience is up in arms against him and the storms of condemnation follow him wherever he goes.

How To Recover From a State of Backsliding

To recover from a state of backsliding:

1. *Remember from where you have fallen.* Face the question at once and deliberately compare your present

state with that in which you once walked with God.

2. *Take a good, honest look at your true position.* Don't put off any longer dealing with the conflict between God and your soul and the differences between God and you.

3. *Repent at once and do your first works over again* (Revelation 2:5).

4. *Do not attempt to get back by merely changing what you do on the outside.* Begin with your heart and immediately get right with God. Give yourself no rest until the question of your acceptance before Him is completely settled.

5. *Do not act like a mere convicted sinner and think you must "reform and make yourself better" before you can then come to Christ.* But understand distinctly that *coming to Christ alone* can make you better! However much distress you may feel, know for certain that until you repent and accept His will *unconditionally*, you are no better and are constantly growing worse. Until you throw yourself upon His sovereign mercy and thus return to God, He will accept nothing from you or from your hands.

6. *Do not imagine yourself to be in a justified state, for you know in your heart that you are not.* Your conscience condemns you, and you know that God ought to condemn you. *For if He justified you in your present state, your conscience could not justify Him.* Come then to Christ at once, like the guilty sinner you are. Own up and take all the shame and responsibility upon yourself, and believe that in spite of all your wanderings from God, He loves you still. He has loved you with an everlasting love, and with lovingkindness is even now drawing you back to Himself.

CLOSING REMARKS

Friend, it is time to hear the loving voice of God and not shove it aside. There is an alarm that is sounding to those who will listen. Time is too short to live haphazardly and then go to hell. He is speaking to hearts, "Wake up," before it is too late.

Hebrews 3:7-14 TLB says:

...the Holy Spirit warns us to listen to him, to be careful to hear his voice today and not let our hearts become set against him, as the people of Israel did. They steeled [set or hardened] **themselves against his love and complained against him in the desert while he was testing them. But God was patient with them forty years, though they tried his patience sorely; he kept right on doing his mighty miracles for them to see. "But," God says, "I was very angry with them,** *for their hearts were always looking somewhere else instead of up to me,* **and they never found the paths I wanted them to follow."**

Then God, full of this anger against them, bound himself with an oath that he would never let them come to his place of rest.

Beware then of your own hearts, dear brothers, lest you find that they, too, are evil and unbelieving and are leading you away from the living God. Speak to each other about these things every day while there is still time, so that none of you will become hardened against God,

being blinded by the glamor of sin. For if we are faithful to the end, trusting God just as we did when we first became Christians, we will share in all that belongs to Christ.

We must rise up and take responsibility to act on the Word of God we've been taught.

Over these past few years, I have grieved deep within as I have watched some around me be knocked off by the enemy through their negligence, lack of self-control and wrong choices because of not listening to the voice of the Holy Spirit within their hearts. We cannot continue to blame the devil for everything, even though he is the author of every evil thing that happens. We must rise up and take responsibility to act on the Word of God we've been taught. Thank God for His mercy and grace. God is so gracious that if He sees an effort on our part, even where we are weak, He will be strong in us and help us to overcome. *Always remember that He is for you and not against you.*

Second Chronicles 16:9 says, **"For the eyes of the Lord run to and fro throughout the whole earth, to show himself strong in the behalf of them whose heart is perfect toward him...."** One minister said the word *perfect* in the Hebrew connotation gives the idea of "one whose heart is pressing hard after God." *The New American Standard Version* says, **"...that He may strongly support those whose heart is completely His...."** *The New International Version* says, **"...to strengthen those whose hearts are fully committed to him...."**

Thank God! His divine help, strength, support and favor are toward any believer who gives himself (or her-

156

self) to Him in total commitment and who is making the effort to press hard after Him. *He then will make up for our weaknesses and mistakes if He sees that we do not want to compromise but are completely surrendered to Him. A daily surrender of our will to His will is required.*

Luke 9:23-26 says:

And he said to them all, If any man will come after me, let him deny himself, and take up his cross daily, and follow me.

For whosoever will save his life shall lose it: but whosoever will lose his life for my sake, the same shall save it.

For what is a man advantaged, if he gain the whole world, and lose himself, or be cast away?

For whosoever shall be ashamed of me and of my words, of him shall the Son of man be ashamed, when he shall come in his own glory, and in his Father's, and of the holy angels.

Our cross is not anything that Jesus already died to redeem us from. *Our cross is obeying Him to do whatever He tells us to do. It will not be easy. It requires that the fleshly nature tendencies* (or works of the flesh) *die in order that the Spirit of God within us can reign.* It requires fear to be replaced with faith so we can stand for Him unashamedly. But the victory is that He is in us and causes us to triumph no matter what we walk through.

Hebrews 12:1-3 says:

Wherefore seeing we also are compassed about with so great a cloud of witnesses, let us lay aside every weight, and the sin which doth so easily beset us, and let us run with patience the race that is set before us,

157

**Looking unto Jesus the author and finisher of
our faith; who for the joy that was set before him
endured the cross, despising the shame, and is set
down at the right hand of the throne of God.
For consider him that endured such contra-
diction of sinners against himself, lest ye be
wearied and faint in your minds.**

There is a great group of witnesses in heaven desiring to see us finish the race. Remove any weights (even
good things that may be time robbers) or sins which
would try to entangle or hinder you. Fix your eyes on
Jesus, the beginning and ending of your faith. Consider
Him Who endured even more than you've endured so
that you don't get weary or mentally tired or even relaxed
and lose heart. *How do you fix your eyes on Jesus? Not
by looking at a picture of Him, but by fixing your mind
on His Word.* He and His Word are one. His Word will
strengthen and help you.

A year ago my husband was preparing to speak to a
Christian men's meeting when suddenly he had a vision
of the saints in heaven on their feet looking over an edge
down upon the earth. They were pressing to see all of the
Christians in this last day finishing the race of life and
time. He said he immediately thought of Hebrews 12:1,
and then he had a flash in his mind of the last quarter of a
ballgame. He was reminded of a team in Texas where, in
the last quarter of the game, all of the people in the stands
stood to their feet and cheered for the team, standing for
the entire quarter. They call it the ninth man on the team.
It is very exciting and intense. Those saints who have
gone on before us are standing and cheering us on.

The Spirit of God spoke within his heart that we are

in the last quarter of time. We are
in the final lag of the race. In the
final lag of the race, they put in the
fastest runners. We are called in
this hour to run the race and usher
in the return of Jesus Christ.

> *We are called
> in this hour to
> run the race
> and usher in
> the return of
> Jesus Christ.*

First Peter 2:9 says:

**But ye are a chosen genera-
tion, a royal priesthood, an
holy nation, a peculiar people; that ye should
show forth the praises of him who hath called you
out of darkness into his marvellous light.**

Choose To Hear God's Voice

John 10:4-5 says that God's sheep hear His voice,
and the stranger's voice they will not follow.

**And when he putteth forth his own sheep, he
goeth before them, and the sheep follow him: for
they know his voice.**

**And a stranger will they not follow, but will
flee from him: for they know not the voice of
strangers.**

I pray this scripture over my life. This doesn't mean
you and I will never hear the stranger speak to us. Believe
me, the stranger (Satan) speaks to Christians and non-
Christians. We must learn to recognize his voice (or his
tactics of temptation, lust, etc.) and resist him.
Remember, his ultimate plan for your life is to destroy
you — spirit, soul and body.

In Revelation, chapters 2 and 3, God is speaking to
seven types of churches. To each church He says, "Hear
what the Spirit is saying to the churches." To one church

He exhorted them that they didn't
love Him as they did at first
(Revelation 2:4-5). He instructed
them to think about those times
of their first love toward Jesus
and turn back to Him again.

> *Our life is
> made up of
> daily choices.
> Those choices
> can bless us or
> destroy us.*

May we not be a part of those
Jesus prophesied about in
Matthew 24:12, that because of
so much sin running rampant everywhere, our love
grows cold toward God and others.

As we review what has been written, we must choose
to be doers of the Word and not hearers only; not quit praying; keep our hearts right in relationship to others; and
give or share what we've received.

Our life is made up of daily choices. Those choices
can bless us or destroy us. Some who read this will have
already made the commitment to guard their hearts and
obey the Lord. Others will be led to recommit to keeping
what has been entrusted to them from God.

Deuteronomy 30:15-16,19-20 says:

**See, I have set before thee this day life and
good, and death and evil;**

**In that I command thee this day to love the
Lord thy God, to walk in his ways, and to keep
his commandments and his statutes and his
judgments, that thou mayest live and multi-
ply: and the Lord thy God shall bless thee in
the land whither thou goest to possess it...**

**I call heaven and earth to record this day
against you, that I have set before you life and
death, blessing and cursing: therefore choose**

life, that both thou and thy seed may live:

That thou mayest love the Lord thy God, and that thou mayest obey his voice, and that thou mayest cleave unto him: for he is thy life, and the length of thy days: that thou mayest dwell in the land which the Lord sware unto thy fathers, to Abraham, to Isaac, and to Jacob, to give them.

If there is any area that you need to repent and turn from, now is the time to do it. If you are ready to choose life instead of death, blessing instead of cursing, good instead of evil, and are ready to make a full commitment of your life to Jesus Christ, Who is righteousness and holiness, and submit to Him, pray with me now. As you pursue Him, abide in Him and He in you, He will expose deception before it has an opportunity to ensnare you. If you have been in deception, you may pray the following prayer which I've written, or you may pray in your own words a prayer of repentance and commitment to follow through with God's principles.

Father, I repent for being apathetic in some areas of my life and for following my own agenda rather than Yours at times. Show me where You want me to attend church and get plugged in to an area of service that will help me grow spiritually, Lord.

Help me to establish a daily time for study and meditation of Your Word and a daily time for prayer. Help me to be rightly related to the Body of Christ. Thank You for opportunities to give out of myself and to witness of Your great love plan, Lord, as I grow in You.

I submit to your lordship, Jesus. Lead and guide me in the way You would have me go, so I can fulfill the des-

tiny to which You have called me.

I hear Your voice, Lord, and I will follow You. The voice of a stranger I will not follow, in Jesus' name. Amen.

ABOUT THE AUTHOR

Sharon Daugherty and her husband, Billy Joe, are founders and pastors of Victory Christian Center, Tulsa, Oklahoma (with a congregation of nearly 10,000 people), which meets in the Mabee Center on the Oral Roberts University Campus.

Raised a Methodist minister's daughter, Sharon made a commitment to Christ and accepted the call of God as a teenager. Music plays an important role in Sharon's life. She ministers in singing and songwriting. She oversees the praise and worship ministry at Victory Christian Center, and has recorded numerous cassettes and CD's.

Sharon teaches in Victory Bible Institute, a weekly Bible Study, and ministers alongside her husband pastorally. Other ministry outreaches in which she and her husband have been involved include a radio and television ministry, now international in scope; monthly crusades in government-subsidized housing projects in Tulsa and the surrounding areas; and overseas crusades where numerous churches and Bible schools have been established.

Sharon's books, *A Fruitful Life: Walking in the Spirit* and *Called By His Side*, are now available. Music tapes which are available include: Now Is the Time, Turn It Around, Stand Your Ground, Healing Songs & Scriptures, We Can Build a Dream With Love, My Folks' Favorites, Somewhere It's Snowing, Covered By His Love (protection songs and Scripture), Exalt the Lord and Prepare the Way of the Lord (two live recordings of Victory Christian Center's praise and worship).

Sharon and her husband have four beautiful children: Sarah, Ruth, John and Paul.